THE WAY BACK HOME

THE WAY BACK HOME

COURTNEY PEPPERNELL

Andrews McMeel
PUBLISHING®

Acknowledgments

As an author, the creation and production of a book is not a journey you take solo; it's a team effort. I have been blessed in my career to have an amazing support network around me—James, Katherine, Byron, Karna, Justin, and all those at Andrews McMeel Universal, notably Patty, Liz, and Diane. Thank you for your support and for all your effort; I could not do this without you. My family, as always, my most precious support network, thank you. And, of course, my readers, you bring me back home, always!

One final note I wanted to make—parts of this book have been inspired by the pandemic, which has changed the world. For months and into the years that followed, we were changed. We felt all sorts of emotions: fear, frustration, anger, sadness, and loneliness. But we also felt courage, grace, and a will to survive. There were many stories that inspired me, and I wanted to share with you some of those feelings I felt while reading them. While I always try to write my books so that you can pick them up time and time again when you need them most, I felt different writing this book; it helped to remind me that, as humans and as people, we are capable of so much more than we think we are. Despite the loss the world has suffered, we, the people, are capable of rebuilding. So, here's to you—may you always find your way home.

Instagram: @courtneypeppernell
TikTok: @courtneypeppernell
Twitter: @CourtPeppernell
Email: courtney@pepperbooks.org
www.peppernell.com

One day, a dark storm fell upon the earth. For days and months, the shadow persisted, and a deep sadness spread across the world, shattering its worth. People lost many things. They lost friends and family; they lost security and freedom and faith as well. But mostly people lost themselves.

So, the world ached, the beat of its heart a little less whole. Many people searched and searched but could not seem to find its lost soul. Until one day, while walking along a beach, waves crashing at my feet and sunlight within reach, I stumbled across a spirit made of seashells and coral, of ocean stories and treasures found in sand dunes, and of gleaming stardust washed onto the shore by the moon. With golden eyes, and wonder from the deep blue, the spirit stared up at me and said,

"I knew you'd find me; a friend told me about you."

"Oh," I replied, "do I know this friend?" and the spirit said, "You may. They exist deep in the forest, guiding seeds, from where once souls grew."

And so, I sat down in the sand, cross-legged and intrigued, and asked the little spirit, "Tell me, how do I find what the world needs?"

Said the spirit in earnest, "After a storm, despite all the destruction in its wake, we must find it deep within ourselves to find a way through such heartache."

"But where to start," I replied, "when one feels so desperate and alone?"

And the little spirit continued, "When mending a soul and the things that entails, we must first build a home, so safekeeping prevails."

"A home?"

The spirit nodded, "A home, to rebuild and to relearn, for once a home is built, all that we are will eventually return."

There on the beach, as the day grew bright, the little spirit handed me a key, with a final note: "To find your way back, start where you are now—this key unlocks the truth of life; have hope!"

So, into the world I ventured, to find and collect all the things that would surely make a home. Like courage for its foundation, despite how heavy fear seems, and support, of course, to uphold the beams. Like strength to steady the floors and grace to restore the walls. Like resilience to open the windows and release all burdens. I unearthed love from the depths of forgotten memories to fuel the fireplace and keep the home warm, discovering in the process my potential to weather every new storm. I found my purpose again, to tend to the garden, reminding the tree roots to take hold and the flowers to bloom, and I made a promise to myself, I would always turn on the light and look for faith in every room.

And in all this building and all this repairing, I learned an important thing. That when you start with every day and choose to carry on, the world's rhythm begins to sing. Until, eventually, the darkness subsides and the water recedes, and you'll find yourself returning like an old friend, lost for a while but never truly gone, a bump in the road but not the end—for even if we fall and become lost in the way we roam, humanity's greatest strength will always be its resolve to find the way back home.

(A) NORTH ELEVATION

(B) EAST ELEVATION

(C) SOUTH ELEVATION

(D) WEST ELEVATION

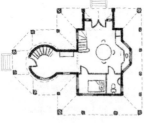

(E) GROUND FLOOR PLAN

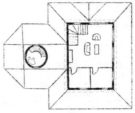

(F) FIRST FLOOR PLAN

MATERIALS

- WOOD
- COURAGE
- TILES
- CONCRETE
- SUPPORT
- PLASTER
- STRENGTH

- GRACE
- CORAL
- RESILIENCE
- LOVE
- SEAWEED
- PURPOSE
- FAITH

ELEVATION DRAWINGS

GROUND + FIRST FLOOR PLANS

Table of Findings

1

To build a foundation
(*find courage*)

36

To uphold the beams
(*find support*)

58

To steady the ground
(*find strength*)

84

To restore the walls
(*find grace*)

114

To open the windows
(*find resilience*)

136

To fuel the fireplace
(*find love*)

174

To tend the garden
(*find purpose*)

200

To turn on the light
(*find faith*)

Find Courage

As with most things in life,
courage is often buried deep
in the quietest corners
of our hearts.

And every so often, one needs
to be reminded that their
courage still exists,
despite the overwhelming fear
or the relentless trauma and
the moments not always clear—
courage still beats within you.

And like most things in life,
the courage will return
to the surface—
like the sun after rain,
the light after darkness,
the forest after the fire,
and the calm after the storm.

It is too simple
for someone to tell you
to manifest courage—
to think about courage
and suddenly
you are courageous,
like it's a magic trick.

There is nothing simple
about courage.

It is not given to you
wrapped in
pretty bows and lace.

It is grit, persistence, a battle.

You find courage by
choosing to step forward,
every day,
even on the days you pause,
or the days you do not
see the progress.

For even in the stillness
of this life,
your existence matters.
Courage lives in the
refusal to surrender
and the will to stay.

For months, I was swallowed by fear. The anxiety held on, clasped across my chest, tightening with every breath. It felt like being at the bottom of a forgotten well. Always trying to climb my way out, but falling, over and over again. One afternoon, standing in the bathroom, lights dimmed, shower still running, I looked at my refection in the mirror, and I said, *Are we really going to carry on, with all this fear inside?* So, I had a conversation with Courage. I told Courage I had lost the fire burning inside my heart—that the world was messy, unforgiving, and in a state of chaos, and it had begun to eat away at me.

Courage looked back at me and said, "I come and go."

"Why," I demanded. "I need you every moment of my life. Why do you always leave me when I need you the most?"

"Because fear needs space too," Courage offered.

And so I looked deeper into the reflection in the mirror, and I saw courage beating within the rhythm of my heart, and I saw fear as well, beating simultaneously alongside it.

"You can always find me," Courage said. "Be at peace with your fear; it runs alongside me, as I run alongside it—fear will not stop you from finding me."

The more life changes, the more you want to push your heels into the ground and stay still. It just feels safer, normal. If you stay there, nothing in life can ever hurt you. If you stay still, so too will all the thoughts. And if your heart hurts, by staying still, it can't get any worse. Like you've frozen the pain in time, and it's the pain you're so familiar with anyway that perhaps it's just easier to let it stay.

You're not hurting anyone; you're not orbiting other lives anymore; you're just stationary, fixed, like a stone statue outside a museum that no one ever really takes the time to notice.

But you're hurting yourself. You're denying yourself the chance to orbit your own life.

When you finally relax your heels and you start to put one foot in front of the other, in a walk, and then a jog, and then a run, it's not like this earthquake of a moment. It's not like life suddenly explodes and there you are. It's softer than that. It's the kind of thing that people only notice if they look closely.

But you notice. You notice the change.

And this breathtaking thing happens; you realize that *you* made it happen. You moved your feet. You had the courage to take the step forward when everything inside you told you not to.

You become this different person; no matter how small the change, you get to be this new person, filled with memory but also filled with possibility.

And there's something truly beautiful about that.

She told me she did not
want to feel anymore,
because life with all the heartache
felt too heavy.

She told me she wanted to run away,
hide somewhere inside herself,
that if she gave in to weakness,
there would be no need to live
with a broken heart.

So I reminded her that living with
her heart open, despite all the ache,
meant she held courage.

That, in time, like all things,
she would once again flourish.

Even inside the darkest room
a light flickers dimly yet determined—
illuminating warmth across my skin.
I am hesitant, and a little unsure.
Still, I find the courage within.

Even when the train does not slow down,
passing forgotten towns and leaving me
alone staring out the window in a daze,
miles from the place I wanted to begin.
Still, I find the courage within.

Even when the doubt crawls into my heart
and creates a home filled with dread,
and I am a whirlwind of reckless thoughts—
losing faith in the day, the night, everything.
Still, I find the courage within.

I had thought that perhaps if the universe intervened, then I would become a different person. That perhaps, then, good things would stay in my life. So, I asked the universe each day to make me different, make me better. But, instead, all I ended up with were empty hands and haunting lessons, just life passing by in a rearview mirror.

It was as though winter returned every morning and refused to soften. The nights were hardest—all that confusion, all that loneliness, who was I, if everything I touched burned? What would I become, if all life meant was a long list of broken promises and not knowing what path to always travel?

It became habit, to sleep in front of the fire, most nights never making it to bed, most days never bothering to get dressed. As if the universe had decided my purpose was to feel lost, helpless. There would be no soul to carry me, no person to lean on, no love to take my face into their hands and promise life would go on.

And yet the crossroad appeared, on a day I had not foreseen—when the winter had set in, the trees stark and barren, the sleet relentless. And while on that day the hope felt as though it had all but faded, in the final moments of dusk, in the glinting rays of the sun, the universe finally spoke to me, and it said that transformation was never easy. That we do not emerge from the darkness by magic or by the universe's intervention. The universe instead had sat on the sidelines, watching, waiting, hoping.

The truth of the matter was this—it was my job to find the courage myself. I was the intervention. I chose what road to travel. I was the good in my life. I needed to create the magic all on my own, even through the fear and in all the ways I had drowned. For in the courage comes this new capacity to be beautiful, brave, and found.

Our world starts and ends in ephemeral moments.
They are rolled into years of hoping and longing.
I am in love and in ache with platforms and airports—
they bring you to me, me to you, but then eventually
they divide us.

My heart settled on yours, under mistletoe and a kiss.
You walked into my run-down town with light in your eyes,
and I was never able to look away, never.

We used to say that an ocean between us
meant I was the sun and you were the moon.
We were an eclipse—beautiful, powerful, spellbinding.

Yet how fleeting an eclipse is, in the scheme of life.
I think more of this, every day, every hour.
You know I will always hold deep hope for us, for you,
but I wonder if someday you'll grow tired.

Since our last moment, it has been a memory on loop,
that day in the departure terminal.
When the world closed.
You had to go back, for months, years, they didn't say—
no one knew.

You turned and looked at me, eyes swollen, smile crooked.
My heart stopped, and you mouthed the words "I love you";
all I could manage was a soft reply, "See you soon."
And since you left, I have spent every moment since
wondering if you will ever return, if we will ever find the other.

Most days, I ask myself how many more ways are there to ache;
is there no end to the unremitting wanting, needing, and missing?
This is what I have always feared—we will remain

forever out of reach.

If I could turn back
the hands of time,
I would tell a younger me
that the person
she will spend the most time
with in life is herself.

I would tell her to be gentle
when looking at her reflection.
I would tell her courage
always remains, even on the
days she cannot see it.

I would tell her there is no shame
in falling apart, that life isn't always
picture-perfect or uplifting.

But I would also promise her
there is always good and necessity
in growing and rebuilding.

There was a time a dark winter set upon the earth,
shadows wrapped tightly around cities, and people
were divided, souls lost, hearts broken in half.
During those months spent in solitude, the world
stopped revolving; long, dark days bled into each other.

In this time, I spent much of the days lost inside my head,
creating this new, untainted world, far away from the real one.
And it wasn't until a particularly bright day that I came home,
untangled my thoughts from my new, safe world, and returned
to the world I had lived in, the world I had always known.

It was on this bright day I discovered an important thing—
that the world I had always known could be beautiful once more,
that people could be better than I had thought them to be before.

Perhaps the answers I had been looking for each and every night—
on how to be brave and find a way to make it through—
existed in all the ways people chose to carry on and find the light.

The maple trees are shedding leaves,
and I am reminded of the beauty
in letting go.

The way the trees rustle and the leaves
fall, and yet the branches remain.

Like shedding layers of skin, only our bones
stay the same, like a house with no walls,
but the structure is still in place,
like the courage I yearn for—

I am hopeful my heart will make space.

I looked for hope almost everywhere, every corner
of the earth. But it had disappeared, and in turn
I had become so truly lost.

One particularly arduous day, my heart was destroyed
again. The little bookshop I had found such solace
within had burned to the ground.

I wept in front of the blackened remains and the
shattered windows,

Where will the stories live now?

I stood on the curbside, for hours wondering where I
would find my solace, my relief, my serenity.

And like the hope I had been longing to find, out
of the ashes a small wildflower appeared.

Still in the midst of sprouting, reaching for the sun.

It was here, after all the searching, I was finally
reminded that, in spite of the fire, and the continual
days not knowing which way to go, sometimes even
a tiny seedling still has the courage to grow.

The uncertainty exists
in every day,
some smaller, like whether
to have coffee or tea,
if the package you ordered
will arrive on time,
what to wear to your
meeting at noon.

Some bigger, like life changes
and loss and not knowing
if the stars will return to the sky
after a dreary day filled with gloom.

But the uncertainty can lead
you down beautiful paths and through
places you never dreamed of venturing.

Life does not end with uncertainty.
There have been beautiful things
discovered in the unknown.

She said
I am retreating
behind my walls

She said
I have been hurt
too many times before

She said
my heart can't
take this anymore

To her, I say—
"Your courage to wear
your heart on your sleeve
is the most beautiful
thing about you."

HAVING HEART

Before everything we knew changed, I had always thought courage came from the people around me. That I was braver because I had my mother to lean on, or my brother to call, or my friends to hold me up. But when the world shut down, and we became separated from all the things we knew and all the people we loved, I was alone. I wondered, every day, where would I find courage if I was alone.

Courage is from the heart. It is the center of us. The reason our blood flows through our veins and our lives carry on. The heart suffers many things—broken from others, grievances of life, rejection, disappointment, overwhelming fear. But it also holds room for joy, love, admiration, and tranquillity. Without having heart, we cease to live.

More importantly, courage comes from having heart.

The Spark

Beyond the rolling mountains and cornfields sprawled a forest—filled with evergreen and cedar trees, dogwood and wildflowers. Far from the trails and by a babbling creek, there was a log cabin, cobwebs strung across the wooden beams, layers of dust on all the windowsills. And in the log cabin, a fireplace, with forgotten picture frames on the mantelpiece. A small spark had lived between the logs, always warming the cabin, its purpose to exist as the heart of the night. But the heart had long been abandoned. Some say the spark had been lost to the ache, that the cabin had become a graveyard, love had perished, and so too had the spark.

One night, as fireflies dotted the woods, a silhouette arrived on the cabin doorstep, holding a lantern. The silhouette pushed open the cabin door and placed the lantern in the doorway. It opened the windows, swept away the dust. It took down the forgotten picture frames and replaced them with newer memories. It stocked the pantry, remade the bed, and fluffed the cushions.

And lastly, tenderly, it lit the fireplace. Smoke billowed from the chimney.

The little spark had returned—warmer than before, stronger, lighting up the night.

The honeybees returned after winter,
swarming around the old tire swing
still hanging in the corner of the yard.
And they asked about you,
like they did every time they returned,
but I told them you had gone,

your memory now as soft as tiny wings
quivering against the now blue sky,

and the honeybees murmured a sad song,
as though they felt the ache in my heart.

Perhaps they miss you as much as I do,

and if only we could return to the
life we had before, smiling and laughing,
the house always warm, sitting on the deck,
watching the honeybees and how they swarm.

I knew the dream had ended on the night
you left, and, in the morning, you didn't return.
Maybe it was the wrong time or the wrong life
and we hadn't figured out all the things to learn,
but I wonder if you caught that train or plane,
the one you said you always would, and you're
someplace else, someplace better.

I'm sorry words failed me and I didn't have
the right ones to say to you in those early hours
one morning, when I called and you answered.

I didn't know what to say.
I'm sorry for the silence.

So many have told me about the newness,
how it will feel when my heart finally catches up.
That I will be a new person, find new love, new life.
But I cannot think of such things yet, without you.
So, for now, I watch the honeybees on my own
as they make their new home again.

You are never the same, not after such loss. It's just like something inside you breaks and it never really heals—not completely. The skin may join again over the wound, but you're still left with a scar. The ache never really goes away; it's a ghost, always returning, forever haunting. It's just, over time, your heart makes room for it. And in the space that it now haunts, the rest of your heart tries to fill itself with the courage to continue forward, compensating for a grief you never thought you would have to live with. It's like breaking your right hand and learning to use your left hand, or losing your sense of taste and relying on the memory you had of strawberries, such sweetness. You grow into the space, and eventually it does not consume you.

I will admit, the courage
is found in many places, but
mostly it is found in the way
time and things change.

The way the leaves fall
and then regrow
from season to season,
much like the way I fall
and rise again.

The way walls become
flaked, chipped, and cracked,
and yet they are painted
with fresh coats to look new,
bursting with all this color—
much like the way I choose
to get dressed each morning
and embrace a new me forever.

The way a building is torn down
after too many holes and leaks
and someone starts all over again,
much like the way I reinvent
my heart and find courage instead.

The world came crashing down, and the days turned into months all blended together in a blur. The nights hurt, but then again most nights do.

And in my dream, there I was, only everything about me was nothing like the way it should be. My hands were not my hands. My eyes were not my eyes. My spirit was not my spirit.

And when I woke, I was afraid. What would become of my soul if I could no longer recognize every part that made me, me.

What would become of my dreams if I could no longer close my eyes.

Outside my window, the sky was clear, and I spoke soft words, reminding the stars how much I needed them.
And they called to me, asked me to embrace the cool spring evening.

So, I stood on the stoop for what seemed like an entire lifetime, a new eternity where the sky had been blissfully reborn, and then—a comet—and the tail end lit up the sky in a way I had never seen before.

I knew I would sleep well, a sign reminding me life crashes in the same way a comet does, but, oh, how it lights up the sky.

Be on this journey with me as I seek the courage to tell the world,
"I love you."
It's changing, I know, but I am still afraid.
Not of our love; I could never be afraid of our love.
But how it is perceived, yes.

It doesn't make sense, I know, because love is so beautiful.

Be on this journey with me as I find the courage to tell the world,
"I am who I am."

Because, truly, I love you.
Not loving you would be the biggest mistake of my life.

FROM THE SUN

It is not a singular event;
to be who you are.
You are always evolving.
You are always seeking
courage to express yourself.

Conformity is soul damaging.
It rots you from the inside,
day by day, year by year.
It stops you from seeing beauty—
from being and relishing beauty.

So, the rain feels heavier, and
the storm rages on inside you.
Shadowing all the good in your life.
Stripping you of light from within.
It is meant to be fought.
I had been so many things before
I had been myself.
I was lost, scared, filled with chaos.
I was angry, alone, devoid of love.
But I was looking for myself in all
the wrong places. I had never existed
in the deep shadows or the darkness.
I had not inherited the dread, I had
allowed it to consume me instead.

I had always been the sun.

To the Moon

All her life, she had dreamed of floating between the stars, of soaring to a place where gravity did not exist. Perhaps here she would find peace. Over the years, the moon had lovingly watched her grow, always listening to her secrets. There was much to be learned about life—like finding strength and integrity, harnessing determination, and discovering her destiny. But there was one lesson that she struggled with, a lesson that took years to transpire. And that was her ability to have the courage to dream, to ignite within a passionate fire. When she finally did find the courage, there were many who tried to stop her, who tried to squash her motivation to strive. But she took these hindrances and spun them into drive. For nothing in the world would stop her from reaching the stars. When the day finally came, it was bright, filled with warm rays of yellow.

Three breaths, inhale, exhale, release.

Two eyes to always look ahead.

One heart to hold on.

The rocket launched, and she looked back at the world, the continents, sea, and sky, now the image of a younger her.

Speaking to the earth, she said, "I hope you find the courage to dream well, my friend."

A Mountain Town

The wheels shuddered to a halt, the steam let out a deep, unapologetic sigh, and the train abruptly stopped. The driver announced a snowstorm, pointed all the passengers to the nearest town, and told us to return in the morning. We trudged through the snow and found ourselves in the corner of a tiny hotel, warming our hands by the fire. We were just meant to be passing through, having rode the train most of the way in silence. Now there was reason to speak, and I could not find the words. My heart was a mess—how could I have held her name so delicately on my lips all that time without whispering it to her in a way I had always wanted to, softly, tenderly, with all the awe I felt for her?

The snow fell softly and thoroughly outside the window, the mountains silhouetted against the fading light of the day. Maybe it was in the way the mountains had looked at me, filled with will, urging me to tell her how I felt. But how could I when there were so many ways to be afraid that I would often count them before I slept? Still the mountains urged—"There is no reason you cannot climb, fly, reach."

Over the amber flames of the fire, I sought all the courage deep within my heart, and I told her the way she looked with sleet in her hair was more beautiful than any work of art. I told her the way she existed in a world alongside me was the closest thing to magic that I had ever seen.

And then her lips were on my lips, her hands were in my hair, breathing a lifetime into my lungs I didn't even know was there.

"I would climb those mountains for you," I said, drunk and in love, "because you make me believe in what I can do."

And with her eyes on mine, she replied, "I would climb any mountain, as long as I was with you."

An honest conversation
one with heart
was all I ever wanted from you—

I wanted all the things you
were too afraid to say
to tumble from your lips
and find a way into my heart

Somewhere in between all the
longing and the fear that kept
us worlds away from each other
we could find a place of courage
a place our hearts could be together

Our place—
always and forever

At Dusk

I am standing on the shoreline
the water edges closer inward
and I am looking at the seagulls
as they fly against the pink sky—

The sun is sinking, a day's goodbye
I am thinking of you, of your heart
And the way it continues forward
every day and all through the night.

For what it's worth, we all experienced the storm in different ways. Some worse than others, but there was a commonality to the isolation. It lay in the monotony of every day. The sun felt as though it did not shine, the sky felt as though it did not sing, the walls felt as though they were always caving in. The loneliness dragged on and on. Even if you shared the same walls as others, you still felt alone. There was too much thinking, too much worrying, too much of all the things you did not want to feel—and yet, despite this monotony, there was light. It came about in the ways most beautiful things come about, in small, wonderful little moments. Like how on every walk there would be windowsills covered in signs wishing the world well. Like how the ones we loved always tried to make us laugh a little harder. Like how every essential worker and first responder pulled the world along, always with a nod to make you feel just that little bit better. The storm did take hold, and it did change us, but it also surprised us, reminded us we can survive the darkness, if we do it together.

I

In late September, a voice is singing from a balcony strung
with laundry. It is a sad song but also beautiful.
Even the birds rest on the windowsill to listen, in unison.
They lend their melodies to the song, and somehow
it carries all throughout the alleyways, searching for
answers, looking for hope.

II

The days feel longer and longer. It has been a difficult year,
this one. Things happened I never thought could. I can see
it in the world's sunken eyes—exhaustion, defeat, all the
unknowns. And yet light still remains inside.

III

I listen to my own heartbeat. Often alone in the dark.
A reminder I am alive.

IV

I promise, I am trying. Really trying. Even on the days
the world seems bleak. Even on the nights all I can muster
is a gentle smile in my sleep.

I trust that
there is purpose
in all the things I feel.

Even if the pain
takes years to heal.

Even if the journey
feels impossible to
explain.

I know that in life
it takes courage
to return home again.

Someone somewhere is still
searching for meaning—
in all the creases of their life.

There is a story they are writing,
and I am desperately listening.
For I too have so much to say.
In the early hours, I speak courage
into my space, insisting it continues
to flourish and rise in my veins.

The stars have forewarned
the ocean can be rough and the
earth can spark and erupt.
Nothing is ever still—time, love,
or any matters of the soul or heart.
The world can be so unforgiving,
a rage deep under the surface skin.

And yet I am still here,
I'm here
and

I carry on.

Find Support

Often, I have found encouragement within the wilderness, the spontaneity and unpredictability of a day in the forest, silent one moment and then filled with life the next. Every step is a step along a path of the unknown. And when looking at the forest, it is easy to only ever see the most glorious and tallest tree. You stare up at this beautiful and transcendent wonder of nature and become lost in all the years it has been here. But a forest is not a forest because of one tree. It is a forest because of many trees. We too are made up of many working parts—and together they carry us forward in life. Pay heed to your heart as equally as your body and your spirit.

I hold your soul
in the palm of my
hands
and I whisper
all the delicate things;
be joyful, be free,
my darling,
and spread your
beautiful wings.

They used to tell me
to hold my tears inside.
To deny those tears
the right to flow.

If you cried or let go,
it made people uncomfortable.

Nobody likes it when you cry.

All those tears streaming down
your face meant only one thing—
that you were not strong enough,
you were too weak to handle all
the things life threw your way.

But then one day, as I cried
alone in the bathroom stall,
locked away and hidden,
someone knocked on the door,
and I opened it, thinking this was
just another person
to tell me I was weak.

But a girl stood on the other side,
tears streaming down her face too,
and she asked softly but defiantly,
"Would it be okay if I cried with you?"

It was in all the watching
that I realized people
have some things in common.

All our longings are the same.

Happiness, hope, adventure, love.

We long to find happiness in
the way we live each day.

We hope to breathe through
every difficult time, no matter
how bad or what people say.

We long for adventure, for new
memories to be made.

And we long for love, for someone
to hold us and always stay.

When you are on the very edge
and staring out into the world,
you wonder how you got there
filled with such grief and dread.

When did life become so jaded
or more difficult to comprehend;
where do you store all the sadness,
and what will make it end?

But then you start to look out,
far beyond your own problems,
and you notice all the others,
a little bruised and a little broken.

All the many scars worn in pride,
and every heart that has shattered,
knowing they'll surely shatter again—
for from life there is nowhere to hide.

Yet you see someone start to pick up
all these broken pieces of themselves,
tenderly and bravely willing to start anew,
and you think, *Perhaps it is possible that
I can pick up all my broken pieces too.*

You must think of yourself like a clock. You are ticking through the motions of every day, moving down the path of life. And because you are a clock, there are many cogs working together to help you move forward. These cogs might be your favorite teacher, your neighbor, your best friend, your family, your child, your favorite writer or actor, musician or dancer. These cogs keep time turning in your world—no matter the sunshine, the rain, or the storm. Without cogs, a clock does not operate.

For all the people who walk into your life, there will be an important few who fill your heart with memories and your mind with a world of possibilities. These are the ones to hold on to, the ones to show how much you care. So, with these few, give them your time. For time is the only thing that cannot be returned. It is the most precious part of you. When you give someone your time, you are saying, here are all the minutes I will never see again, and they will always be linked with you.

They wonder why we need big parades filled
with color and confetti or a month dedicated
to asking for recognition and empathy.

And to them, I do not respond in anger or
affliction, even if sometimes it feels like the
easier thing to do.

Instead, I ask, if you could not hold the hand
of the person who put stars in your heart or
were cast a look of distaste for simply
expressing yourself in a way that feels like art.

If you did not have the freedom to kiss the one
you love, in front of all those whom you knew, then
you would be marching too, wouldn't you?

Here we are, just a someone in a world of others, a beating pulse inside a universe that goes on forever, a drop of magic in the ocean we call life. Yet, we seem to hold on to this strange narrative—that everything in our lives must be picture-perfect. We must hold the grandest parties and have the most impressive cake; we must have the fancy car and beautiful house; we must have all the answers as parents or learn lessons once and never repeat mistakes. The things we own define us more than the way we hold ourselves. The picture we paint is that nothing can go wrong; there is no blade out of place in the lawn on which we lay our lives.

But there is no truth in this narrative—and the people who matter most know this.

These are the people who walk into your house, see the toys strewn all over the floor, the dishes piled as high as the ceiling, the laundry everywhere, your hair messy, clothes unkempt, eyes a little swollen and puffy, and they never say a thing. Instead, they will ask you about a cup of tea, how your day is, and if you need anything.

That is the kind of story you are worth, where life is not picture-perfect but filled with scribbles and torn pages and a map of a journey having been lived in honesty.

Why didn't anybody warn me how much it hurts
to lose a friend? Why didn't anybody tell me I'd
be up all night, all week, every weekend?

There are all these things to remind me that you don't
come around anymore. What am I supposed to do with
your pictures plastered all over my bedroom wall?

Do you think about every midnight, when we drove around
in your car, listening to songs, going nowhere in particular,
just taking in life aimlessly? What am I meant to do now
that my passenger seat is empty?

What happens to all this space in my life, with your vacancy?

Everybody always asks me how you are, because wherever
they saw me, you weren't very far. What do I tell my mom,
who keeps asking me when will be the next time we're going
dancing at the bar?

I see something that makes me laugh and send it to you, because
I know it would make you laugh too. But I haven't texted
you in months, and I don't know how to go back.

This is the kind of ache I don't know how else to show, because
I miss you so much more than you could possibly know.

The end of my life will come one day, as will yours. There is no escaping this; life happens and then it's over. But these are the things I hope I've done well along the way: I hope I have loved myself in a way that I have loved others, in earnest and with devotion and compassion. I hope I have gone all in, no stone unturned, mountain unclimbed, trail not blazed—and my way too. I hope I have understood the value in good people around me, how precious that is, how important it is to cultivate such relationships. I hope I have picked up the phone more than ignoring it; I hope I have realized that fear and anxiety are nothing to be ashamed of, that these are the things that hold so many of us back, but they cannot conquer us. I hope I have reminded people of their potential, that I have not brought others down. I hope I have inspired people to grow, to know their heart, to come home and be found. I hope I have lived adventurously, even if life can be unpredictable and we don't always know what is around the bend. I hope, through it all, I've been someone to lean on—that I've been a good friend.

For some people, having confidence comes naturally.
They do not know what it is like to be without it.
But for others, they've never known what it means to
have even a drop of it.

I will tell you what it is like, to second-guess everything
that you do—it's a racing pulse and a mind that never seems
to switch off. It's checking something over and over again
and asking for someone else's assurance even though you
know you are good at what you do. It's hearing so many good
things about you, yet all it takes is one slither of negativity
and you bring yourself undone. It's never knowing how
to respond to praise without wondering if the person even
meant it. It's still waters, wanting to let a current take you
forward over moss-stained rocks and out into the wonder of
the ocean but having an eternal fear that the ocean will spit
you back out. That you are unwelcome.

So, for every time you are given the chance to instill even a
drop of confidence in another, do it. There is nothing more
beautiful than watching someone build themselves piece by
piece, embrace the current of their life, rush to the ocean,
and find their freedom.

You will realize it one day. If you blink, you may even miss it. But you will come to understand that the joy of life does not exist in the things we think it does. It does not matter how many possessions we own or how impressive we seem on paper. It does not matter all the hours we devote to becoming better than someone else or all the ways we try to seem more important than another. Because, in the end, we all leave the world for someplace neither you nor I really know. But we leave. And in our wake, it is often not the things we amassed we wish to be remembered for. Instead, it's how often we held out our hand for someone else, it's how many times we thought of putting someone else's needs above our own, it's how many moments we spent giving instead of taking. The joy of life exists in all the ways we support each other.

We look for the people
we once loved in the eyes of others—
will they see me as I was seen before?

But we forget, we are never seen the same way.

We are always restarting
and renewing.

We are born again with every goodbye,
in the same way the sun begins again each day
for the sky.

The world is meant
for building each other
into castles, for holding
each other in times of
duress and struggle.

We are not meant to
burn each other to the
ground.

If we cannot support
each other in the times
we need to come together,
we will be left in ashes.

Time moves forward, and the world continues to spin, and so too do our lives. People arrive and they depart, as easily as ships sail into the bay and leave the very next day. Some trees grow in the opposite direction of each other, some flocks of birds choose to fly south, yet one breaks rank, choosing to go north instead. We don't always remain in the lives of the people we meet, and they don't always remain in ours. But the memories always stay—like the first sunset from on top of the highest hill you've ever climbed and the sky burns in colors you've never appreciated before. And it's all because it's the first time you are sharing the sky with someone you love. The first time you drive hours from home and you're singing lyrics with people who know them line for line, just like you do. The first time you tell someone a secret you'd only ever admitted in your diary, and so they share a secret back, and you feel understood, like someone in the world shares in the same feelings you have. These moments are the reason you are who you are, no matter where you go or where you end up. Even if life changes season to season, the moments have changed you in some way, and all the memories give us reasons.

I hope you find
support
in the same way
the night sky
found the stars.

So, for every time
you feel alone,
you know you
are surrounded
by light.

There is a heartache people speak of,
the kind that keeps them up at night.

Someone took their heart and broke it,
and now they have no idea how to
continue on. They spend all these sleepless
nights staring blankly at a bedroom wall,
wishing that person would just call.

I stare blankly at the wall too,
but nobody broke my heart—I am just sad.

How do you comfort your heart when there
is no reason, no "how" or "why" or "because"?

How do you explain to someone else,
my heart is broken, but I did it to myself?

THE TRUTH OF MARRIAGE

Marriage is not easy. It's not always beautiful and simple and rewarding. It can hurt, it can be teeth gritting and tempers flaring, it can be ugly. You see the best of someone one day and the worst of them the next. It's like standing on either end of a balancing beam, trying to stay steady, but neither person on either end can speak. But it's also uncovering someone, layer by layer, in a way that no one else will. It's having someone in the world whom you want to be with wherever they go; even if you have an argument that morning, no matter where they are, you'll always follow. It's always having a seat saved next to someone. It can be a whole life lived in one day, because that's how connected you feel. It's every bodily function at the most inappropriate of times but laughing about it until the tears roll down your faces. It's whining to someone when you are sick, and even if they grumble back at you, they still make you the soup and hold you anyway. It's having this person to support you on every single mountain you climb, every fire you need to extinguish, and every winter you must survive. They are right there, right behind you or in front of you or beside you; their soul just envelopes yours. It's giving your whole self to someone for all your life and knowing it's finally safe. The truth of marriage is that it's not easy, but when you look at that person, all you see is forever, and you know you have found a love that covers you completely.

You are the home—
within the home are many
important things.

Like the light bulbs,
eyes in the dark, always there
to guide the way.

Like the rooms, compartments
to store the memories and
feelings we share and experience
along the journey.

Like the fireplace, the heart,
every pulse keeping the home
beating.

And perhaps the most meaningful,
but always overlooked—for they are
often hidden by brickwork and panels
and other pretty decor—the beams,
our support, whichever and whomever
they be, hold us up in the moments
when we feel as though our home
may crumble.

Find Strength

As you live and as you breathe, there will be moments the earth shatters. You will crumble, in the same way buildings do in earthquakes. Even if you live each day as though you were made of stone and steel, life will still break you, and suddenly you will wake up and there will be cracks in the ground beneath you. And you'll wonder how they got there, and if there is any way to fill them in. The truth is, we can try all we like to fill the cracks, but they will still cave in every time the earth shatters.

And yet we still build houses over fault lines. We still build cities on ground that will break. This is the same for lives; they go on even when the ground beneath us shatters. But we rebuild, and we go forward, because we were made to have strength; even in the earth-breaking moments when it feels we cannot go on, our strength lies in all the cracks. By knowing this, it is how we steady the ground beneath us. It's how we go on and how we rebuild.

Sometimes you just have to
look at someone as though
they were the only love
you have ever known.

And you have to carry
their heart as though it were
the only heart you've
ever carried.

Sometimes you just have to
choose strength even on the days
when all the walls are caving in.

And you have to wake up in the
morning and choose to live
as though you have never fallen.

The day is still clear to me; it was warm, early September, the month of change—September always seems this way. And we met, at our favorite place, and you told me of how your heart had been broken. Your eyes had filled with tears and disbelief, for you had never once thought this person would hurt you like this. And what could I do? I never believed they would break your heart in two.

And from that day, I had to watch as your entire world fell apart, and it took you along with it. Buried you underneath so much rubble, some days I could not find you. There was nothing I could do to stop the breaking. Believe me when I say I wanted to. I felt anger for the pain you felt, anguish for the ache that sat in your heart, misery for the way you would never be the same again. I didn't want to watch as you went through this pain.

Yet a new September circled back around, and we found ourselves at our favorite place again. Only, this time, you held yourself in a way I had never noticed. With strength and dignity and a fire behind your eyes.

Here is to you and all the Septembers of change.

People always say that you gain strength from your first heartbreak. I think this is true, I do. But I also think you gain more strength from every heartbreak you experience after the first. Because once your heart breaks for the first time, it teaches you lessons about boundaries and the things you deserve. And you tell someone this, and you think they listen, but then they break your heart anyway. So, again, you learn a new lesson. You continue this learning with every new heartbreak, and you continue growing stronger, more in tune with the way you live in the world, more in touch with what you believe love to be. Your heart grows stronger too, knowing what it wants and what it doesn't. So, you do gain strength from your first heartbreak, but I think you gain even more from the second or the third.

You were here one moment and gone the next, and in your absence I learned of many ways grief is described—heavy, empty, silent, loud, fragmented, and full. But I did not know how to sit down with my grief; it moved with me wherever I went. It was too big. There I was, still here, without you, living in a world we had made together. What was I without you? How would I continue on in a life that no longer included you? I felt robbed by death, as though it were a thief, stealing the very thing that breathed life into my lungs and faith into my heart. So I became angry at death; I burned at the very thought of death. And, in time, as though to answer such grief and despair, Death met me by the sea, where the light touched every part of the sky, and to Death I asked, "What will now become of me?" To Death I pleaded, "When will the grief end, before it completely consumes me?"

By the sea, as the tides washed and pulled the world away, Death replied, "I am grief. Here you are, closer to me than you have ever been, and your soul is still beating within."

Death took my hand gently and whispered, "You live in your grief, but you also live through it."

So, here I am,
and I am made of
stardust and thoughts
and skin and feelings.

Sometimes I am
happy and other times
I am sad. All the days,
I am quiet and longing
to spread my wings
and fly high into the sky,
where dreams are endless
and possibility awaits.

I am tired of living my life
the way others wish for
me to live. I cannot change
where I have been or
what I have done, but I can
press onward—
I can find new colors and
create new roads to follow.
I can still wake up each day
and choose to move forward.

I have mourned
my strength many times,
wondering where it goes
in the moments I need it most.

But time and time again,
I am reminded,
it is my strength that mourns me
in the moments I become lost.

I have often imagined people as safety pins. We thread ourselves through the motions of life, trying to hold together those moments and the people we love. And others rely on you to hold their moments together too. But we forget that we all have a sharp point. And in this sharp point exists anger, fear, sadness, and all the things that make us worse than what we really are, all the things that make us doubt our ability to hold our lives together. These feelings will turn up on our doorstep uninvited but walk in anyway. But this does not mean we can't hold ourselves together. The sharp point of a safety pin is connected to the body, and together they hold things in place. This is the same for us; all of the reasons you doubt yourself and your spirit are the very things that pull together with all the most promising strengths about you.

We grieve things in this world,
some more than others.

We grieve when a cloudy sky covers
the stars we have longed to see.
We grieve alone on the bathroom floor,
having lost an opportunity that meant
everything and more.

We grieve a love that changed us
the moment it ended.
We grieve the things that change us
and the memories that break us.

We grieve people we've never met
and the moments we were never given.

But there is a grief that makes me ache
in a way I cannot always explain,
and that is the grief of watching someone
who deserves every beautiful thing
in this world but who does not have
the strength to see it themselves.

It was not the end
of the world
when you broke my heart;
things carried on,
days continued moving,
flowing, beating.

But it was the end of me.

You broke me in a way
I did not ever foresee.
And for every night,
awake at 3 a.m., I doubted
I would ever
open my heart again.

But a curious and wondrous
thing happens when you are alone.
You start to force the impeding,
aching thoughts down.

You squash them, making them
smaller and smaller, until
they can fit into the
palm of your hand.

So, when my ache was tiny,
insignificant, and unimposing,
my heart finally found meaning
in what it meant to persist,
and I realized that a stronger me
would always exist.

I think the idea
is that you can hear
the silence.

It asks you questions—
Are you good enough?
Will you find your way?

And lately I have found
I am speaking back.
Yes, I am good enough.
Yes, I will find my way.

One month, I went away for too long; I had intended to return, but I stayed away. Before I had gone, I had left my plants out by the driveway. The word was that a storm had rolled in, dark and angry and unrelenting. It rained for weeks on end; it did not let up. And my plants drowned. When I finally returned home, it took months to forgive myself. And in that time, I realized, it was not myself I needed to forgive; it was not even that I needed to forgive the rain. Because my plants regrew. What I needed to understand was that they'd had the strength all along, no matter the storm or how much rain fell, or how long I had been gone. And I too have such vigor.

There was Doubt, and it existed in the deepest parts of my heart, and then there was also Strength, who needed room to exist too.

One day, we sat all together on a bench at the train station. Doubt sat on my left, and Strength sat on my right. The train would be coming soon, traveling forward along a journey that only belonged to me. But I did not know which one to bring. Doubt, because it always seemed part of me, or Strength, because I would always need it.

Doubt cleared its throat, speaking to me. "Don't bring me," it said. "If I become too big in your heart, I will take up too much space."

Strength shook its head. "But if you don't come, who will be here to remind us of our limitations, of our boundaries—who will be here to guide us in making better choices?"

Doubt thought on this for a moment. "I don't know," it said. "I think you are better off without me."

The train arrived, and Strength and I stood, boarding. I looked back at Doubt, still on the platform.

The whistle blew, but the train did not move.

Strength hummed beside me, calling out to Doubt. "Don't you see?" Strength said. "Life is the train, and it will not move forward without you. We are intertwined together."

Doubt looked at Strength and then at me. "Are you sure?"

I nodded. "If I do not doubt, then I cannot find strength to believe I can move forward."

So, Doubt boarded the train, and together with Strength, we left the platform.

In the wilderness, across desolate plains and mountain ranges, lived a pride of lions. And in this pride lived the eldest brother and the youngest brother. The eldest brother was strong and vigorous in his approach to life. He was so powerful, he could lift boulders and throw them with little effort. "I am the strongest," he would say to the pride. "I have the strength of one hundred suns."

The youngest brother was not at all like this sibling. He was scrawny, had barely grown into his mane, and could not lift boulders at all. The youngest brother, however, collected letters.

One week, the eldest lion held a performance: how many boulders he could lift and throw all day. The other lions in the pride lay about lazily to watch him. He lifted boulder after boulder, showing off all the muscle and strength that he had. All the while, the younger lion read over his letters.

Soon, tired from all the lifting, and disappointed with how little attention this brought from the other pride members, the eldest lion asked his brother, "Why do you collect all these letters?"

The younger brother explained that the letters contained the hopes and dreams of all the other lions in the pride.

Sometimes power is not measured by how many things you can carry in your arms or on your shoulders but rather the strength it takes to open yourself up and listen to others.

My life felt like the hands
of a compass in the middle
of a solar magnetic storm,
spinning one hundred miles
a minute and unable to settle.

But then I saw you—
and your tenacity for life and
all the beauty of the world
helped me to find my way.

May you be held
in the same way
that the morning
holds the sun,
so that each time
you rise, you have
the strength to
light the day.

Just because I choose to be brave
does not mean I don't feel fear.
Just because I am filled with hope
does not mean I don't doubt.
Just because I wish good things
to happen does not mean they will.

But I suppose there is purpose in all
the mantras and manifestations of the
world, the words that we read, and we
feel something because of it.

We see ourselves in these words.

We see ourselves being brave,
holding hope and carrying forward.

And if you see yourself doing these things
enough, then the ache of reality won't
be too much of a burden to bear.

You can carry on, knowing that even if words
don't always create the resolve,
they are enough to keep you fighting for one.

It was the summer before last,
and I decided to do more gardening.
I wanted to fill my garden with color
and have the butterflies settle on my doorstep.

So, I filled a watering can and watered the garden,
but I forgot to refill the can before retiring inside.

The next day, I reached for the watering can,
 but it was empty.

It is rather simple; I cannot water the garden
if the watering can is empty.

This is the same for you and your support for others—
you cannot support others in their own growth
if you do not have the strength yourself.

You need to remember to fill the watering can.

The year felt stolen from right out under us, filled with isolation and burying too many in graveyards, smiles always hidden and bodies to remain six feet apart. Where to draw strength if we could not stand side by side? But in that year, I lived many lifetimes. For I realized an entire lifetime could be found in all the simple things I had forgotten. Before that year, I had traded nights outside under the stars for hours on my phone. I had traded looking at the person I loved and counting the freckles across her nose for looking at a computer screen. I had traded sitting cross-legged on the lawn with the sunlight on my face for too many moments locked in my office. I had traded more time at the dog park throwing a ball for a rush to check my emails. So even if that year we struggled—and the light at the end of the tunnel always felt as though it were changing, moving farther and farther away—I was still reminded of what was important to me every day. Being here, living, watching, holding on to every moment.

There is no honor in treating someone as though they do not matter, no dignity in silencing those who wish to speak, no joy or resolve in walking away from someone in need of open arms. The truth of life is that it can be a precarious bridge to walk, filled with miles of rotting wood, and you're unable to clearly see the dangers that lurk ahead. We do not know of the things a person has gone through to get to the bridge in the first place. Greatness comes from helping others to cross the bridge, even if you have your baggage too—we are always stronger together.

One year, too many things went wrong. There was so much grief, it was everywhere. At my lowest, I needed relief, so I frequented many places, and I cried there: the corner of the library, sheltered by aisles of books with worlds I'd rather be in; the park bench down the street, with the view of the lake; the bike trail along the beach, with the woody foliage growing along the edging; the parking lot behind the grocery store, where the lights shut off at midnight and plunged me into darkness, although the shadow never seemed to leave. The story was sad, yet it still needed to be lived.

Then, over time, I started to regain my strength. So, I returned to each place: the library, the park bench, the bike trail, and the parking lot—all the places where months before I had cried my heart out. And I chose to laugh and to feel joy in these places instead. I read books that made my heart swell, and I fed the ducks by the lake, and I rode the trail and counted all the new blooming flowers, and I sat in the parking lot with my coffee. I took these places back, for they were no longer places I had been broken in; they were places I had returned to, stronger, and I shared this strength with them.

I rewrote the story.

Perhaps the walls around your heart were not built to keep others out but rather to determine the ones who would be willing to scale the wall. And all the ones who reached the top and peered over long enough to see the heart inside were the ones you could count on. The ones that would have the strength to lift you up in the moments you needed them.

I have known failure; I know failure, and I will continue to know failure. You think that with abounding success comes the end of all your shortcomings, trials, and tribulations, but this is not the truth.

I fail every single day.

I fail when I spill the coffee all over the rug. I fail when I forget to take the dog for a walk, pick up more milk, or put the trash cans out on garbage day. I fail every time I make rash decisions or rush into something, ignoring the risk. I fail when I raise my voice at the people I love and cave into frustration in my career. I fail when sentences are jumbled and I choose the wrong words. I fail when I don't read the instructions first or I don't plan ahead. I fail when I give up instead of finding a way through.

But strength lies in my ability to refuse this failure power.

And it is your strength too. The truth of success is really in the way you say no to failure. Even if it knocks on your door every morning. You allow failure to walk into your home, and, no matter the mess it creates, you carry on with your day, your week, your life.

So, make another cup of coffee, walk the dog, get the groceries, write, forgive yourself, and continue moving forward.

Because, even despite your failures, you will find the way through.

Find Grace

The trees looked sad, the only whispers
through the leaves of grief and despair.
The birds did not sing.
The roads were empty; long stretches
of highway sat in silence.
           The people did not have a pulse.
The stones no longer skipped across water
but sunk to the bottom, tangled in weeds,
lost in the murkiness of misery.
But there was still hope, there was light,
there was empathy.
And I found it in a place I did not expect.
           People's eyes.
The world had begun to speak with their eyes.
I would see it in every passing encounter.
Even though we could not touch, our eyes
became a language, and I heard the world
more clearly as it said—
We are not alone in the way we feel;
we are together.
And, *We can do this; let's take this day by day.*
           And my favorite:
You must stay strong now; everything
is going to be okay.

It begins with a house, and inside the house lives someone I used to know, and within her a beating beautiful heart. This heart, you see, was always thinking of others and putting their needs before her own. Over time, she had learned that compassion was not a one-time thing; it was not something that could be written on a piece of paper and left in a pocket. It was an entire library to immerse yourself within, each day and all days becoming interwoven. Through this, she learned something even more important: that compassion for others was as beautiful as compassion for yourself. So, within her home that welcomed all was also a message painted on the walls—"I belong to me before anyone else."

THE BADGER AND THE SHREW

Years ago, among the rolling hills and wildflowers, on the edge of a sprawling forest, lived a small shrew. The shrew lived a good life. There was lots to forage in the forest and many things to keep the shrew busy. One early evening, as the sunlight dipped low and the forest floor came alive, the shrew heard a cry. Nose twitching, ears alert, the shrew stumbled upon a badger, its leg tangled in a rope and trapped by a fallen tree. "Someone, please help me," the badger called into the evening. "I am trapped."

The shrew thought soberly underneath the cover of mangrove ferns, *If I were to let the badger go, it may eat me right here and now. What to do, and how to be, when a foe calls for help but fear stands in the way? What does that say about me?*

With a deep breath and a timid twitch, the shrew scurried over to the badger and began to gnaw through the rope until, after a moment, the rope fell free and the badger was able to crawl out from underneath the confines of the tree.

The badger looked bewildered, but grateful too. "I will never forget this," said the badger. "Such kindness shown from you."

Spring turned into winter, and the leaves fell, the skies grew darker, and the air turned frosty and cold. The shrew had been preparing for winter—gathering enough food and digging a tunnel to keep warm and dry. But what the shrew had not foreseen was a dark storm approaching, and when the skies opened and the rain fell, the water filled the tunnel, destroying all the work the shrew had done.

Alone, exhausted, and cold, the shrew did not know where else to go; winter was here, and the frost would show no mercy to the forest or the critters below. And then, out of the woods appeared the badger, and the shrew tensed in fear. But the badger looked fondly at the shrew. "You can share my home," the badger said. "I will keep you warm." "Why?" wondered the Shrew. "What has ignited such reform?" And the badger smiled. "If it weren't for your kindness, I would not be here today, so in turn I will shelter you from this storm."

There are just some things that I am unable to do—

I am unable to walk across water or spread my arms
and fly across sunken craters. I am unable to understand
all the languages of the earth or create constellations in
the sky, no matter their beauty or worth.

I am unable to move mountains with my bare hands or
carry home all the seashells found on our walks through
yellow sand.

But I am able to set picnics at your favorite place by the sea
and hold open my arms for you, any time you may need me.

I am able to speak to you in a way that you will always
understand (always saying what I truly mean) and hold your
heart in the same way stars hold hopes and dreams.

I am able to call to the mountains, thankful for this life
worth living, and give the seashells a message more in-depth
than any love letter written.

There are just some things on this journey we call life that I
will not always be able to do, but I will spend every mile of it
being kind to you.

There are forces in this world that want you to stay angry, to think that most people are not kind, or good, or just. Because if you are fueled with hatred, you are blinded to the truth—hatred has not solved any problems; it has only caused them. What to do when all you feel is frustration for the whole wide world? I have found the answer is in the ordinary. Someone holding open the door or helping to retrieve bags from the overhead locker; someone walking hand in hand with the person they love, stopping to dance in the rain. A family laughing together over lunch, a father playing ball with his child in the park, a grandmother making fresh bread, two moms eagerly waiting for the kids to finish school, a concert with live music, when you look at the stranger next to you and know that everything about this moment is cool. People are just people, at the end of the day, and we can find grace in each other, despite what so many others try to say.

It was all the quiet that was
so difficult to reason with.
The silence made life harder.
For in the unequivocal stillness,
the doubt was so much louder.

And I thought to myself,
How am I going to get through
the weeks, months, or years
if these thoughts remain cruel
and callous, refusing me grace—
an unending war with my mind?

So, I decided to make lists.
I made a list every day.
And on these lists, I would write
something kind about a part of me.
The lists did not have to be long,
they did not have to go into detail,
but they had to have a kind word.

I wrote to my heart and to my soul;
I wrote to my mind and to my body.
I wrote to my eyes, my hairline,
my freckles, my wrinkles and scars.
And I told every part of me that I was
loved, that even in the silence and
the doubt, I still had reasons to live.

I was not always this way—able to choose compassion
instead of animosity, able to choose generosity instead
of greed, able to choose kindness instead of callousness.

Even now, so many years after I found grace in a field
of tall, blossoming amaranth, I still return, season
after season, and I ask them, "How do I show kindness
to others even on the days it is not returned to me?"

And every time I ask such a thing, the amaranth
speak among themselves, the cool breeze of a
renewing spring whispering between petals and leaves—

They say to me—when you choose kindness, you will
see a flicker of something in someone's eyes. It is a hint
of gratitude or a hint of surprise.

Gratitude for those who have seen such kindness before
and always welcome into their hearts just a little bit more.
Or surprise for those who have never been met with a
gracious word or smile and now consider such things to be
worth their while.

For even in moments of such conflict, while none of us
can even hope to be perfect, we can hope to be kind,
to choose grace and carry such compassion into every space.

These roots of me
go so deep,
sometimes
I get lost trying
to find a new path

but this heart of mine
holds a home for grace
and anyone's soul who
may need a new start

Maybe "tolerant" is not the word
I have been looking for—
to tolerate is to allow.
But who am I to allow?
I am not the universe;
I am not the decider of all things.

I am a spectator on a stage
that the world lights up.

Perhaps the kinder word is "acceptance."

For to accept is to open arms wide,
to say, "We are different, but this is beautiful.
We are not all made the same,
but this is the beauty of life."

My whole life, I have been met with two doors to two outlooks on life. The first is not to give unless given to, and the second is to give without ever expecting anything in return. I have stood in front of these doors, and I have opened both many times. People have said, "Do not show kindness to someone who will not show it to you." For many years, I thought that perhaps this was sound advice. Still, there was always a pull to the second door, dull, strong, or otherwise, and not until recently did I realize what this pull was—joy. For even if the easier door is to only give when given to—less heartache, less disappointment—I have found that giving without expectation brings me joy. And it is a joy that stays with me, even if the giving is not returned.

I looked at you
and wondered
if anyone had ever
shown you the
same kindness you
had always
shown the world.

Who was there to
hold you, kiss you,
remind you that there
was enough magic in
your eyes to light up
the darkest night?

We are always waiting and hoping for tomorrow;
perhaps then we'll be less impatient or less selfish;
perhaps then we'll find happiness instead of sorrow
and pay more attention to those we truly cherish.

But we lose ourselves in waiting for the next day
instead of seizing the one we are given right now.
We forget the cost of wishing all those years away
and overthinking all the what, the why, and how.

And while I may not hold all of life's cryptic answers,
if we spend less time saying, "I'll get to that tomorrow,"
and living more in the moment and taking chances,
then we'll have more to live for in the time that follows.

Sometimes you have
to respond with grace,
even when the other does not.

Sometimes you have
to open your heart,
even though it has been broken.

Sometimes you have to
choose courage,
even though you are afraid.

One day by chance, or perhaps fate—
I have never truly decided—
I met a dying man at the train station.
We didn't speak for a long time,
until he asked softly,
"Do you think the train will be on time?"

From here, we spoke of the weather,
how it was changing rapidly this fall,
and then we spoke of more meaningful
things like the color of a sunset and
how compared with the entire universe,
we are just so small.

He told me he was sick, but he had learned
to be at peace, for something that he had
studied along the way meant his soul
would eternally rest when released.

He said to me with ease, "The most important
lesson from life, the thing to remember each day,
is to stop and see yourself
in all the people who pass your way.

Find the curve of your smile in the woman
who makes your coffee as a new day breaks
or your sense of adventure in the man
out there fly-fishing by the lake.
Find your warmth in the family that visits
the beach all together and the couple
that goes by them, wholeheartedly in love, forever.

For if you are paying attention, you'll find
we aren't all that different at our core,
and if you see yourself in others,
perhaps you'll learn to love them
a little more than before."

I have slept in the sheets of those before you,
and I have kissed lips that were not yours
and held hands that did not belong to you.

And it was beautiful; they were beautiful.

But it was never like the way it is with you.

You unraveled me in a way that cast all my
inner thoughts and dreams to the light.

All the parts of me I couldn't love, you chose
to love fiercely, with so much more.
All the reasons I thought I was not worthy,
you showed kindness to instead.

This is why I gave you my heart—
because you asked for every part of it.

The world undid me—for so many reasons.
Mostly the truth, because the truth hurts us.
Badly.

Once upon a time, fairy tales were as real as the
magic of sunlight seeping through windows.

And then you grow a little more and suddenly
the world is more difficult, more complex, untrusting.

There are so many days I am misunderstood—
isn't this the kind of thing that can ruin you?

The never-ending loneliness. The want to turn
and run but always staying still.

They tell us all the time, "It's never enough."
You are a ghost of the people you never became,
wasted unwanted potential.

And yet, they do not account for the real magic.

The person who walks into a room and says,
"I will steal stars for you."

And, of course, you know they won't,
because nobody can steal stars, but just that thought—

Someone out there would want to steal stars for me—

It gives you back all your reasons.

If the dandelions can
release their delicate seeds
into the wind and far beyond
settling across barren fields
and growing to create color
then I too can dance through
life with all the grace I have
to always be better.

Splitting at the seams and opening your heart does not feel good. Unraveling and taking down walls takes work. It isn't comfortable to say, "Here I am. What do you think?" But we will always be fighting this battle. We will always be splitting, unraveling, and then trying to put ourselves back together again. The kindest thing you can do is to award yourself grace in these moments. And on the days the grace feels farther and farther away, know that I fight these battles alongside you; we are fighting together.

There were two separate worlds, and in the first world, two friends spent all their time together. One of the friends dreamed of becoming a dancer. She would picture herself dancing across stages and in cities filled with bright lights. But the other friend told her these dreams were not wise, that dancing and searching for lights in lost cities would never get her anywhere. So, the first friend gave up on these dreams. She went a safer route. One with less unpredictability, more routine. And now, each time a dance troupe comes to town, or bright lights glitter in the city, her heart breaks, filled with a deep and irreparable sadness.

In the second world also lived two friends. They too spent all their time together. Again, one friend dreamed of becoming a dancer. She would practice every day, always talking to her friend about the cities she would dance in and the lights that would spell out her name. And this friend listened, always encouraging, every day reminding her to continue dancing.

"You can do this," the friend would say to her. "I will always support you."

And one day, the dreams of the first friend did come true.

There she was, dancing across a world stage, and the friend who had been there from the beginning was in the front row, staring proudly up at the person they'd always loved and known.

It matters how you treat someone, the way you show grace to their dreams, how you hold hope for their passion, how you encourage them to believe. It matters that you are the friend who supports their dreams.

So many times,
you have called in tears,
heart shattered against the wall.
Promising me you will find
silver linings within this fall.
Assuring me another broken heart
doesn't mean you are not fine.
But I can hear the defeat
just by the sound
of your voice on the other line.

So empty, so hollow.

And it is the one thing I wish
you could see clearly,
that even when sometimes in life
we hit rock bottom,
this doesn't mean
that you are something
to be forgotten.

That you are not worthy of the love
you so want to share with someone.

But, beautiful girl, you keep choosing
the wrong heart.

More often the needs of the others
you put before your own.

The most graceful thing you can do
is patch up your broken heart's home.

We measure so many things—
the speed of light, the distance
from one house to the next,
the inches we are in height.

But often we forget to measure
how many I love yous we say
before time quickly passes us by
or how many people we share
honest conversations with, knowing
we all exist under the same sky.

We measure how far we've come
by how many more miles we can run.

We measure how much we've grown
by a mark on the wall with our name.

But how far we've come should
be measured in what we choose
to do with all our time,
and how much we've grown
should be decided
by always choosing kindness,
and not merely sometimes.

For greatness is not measured
in all the things you can do
but by the grace that you show
to all those in need of you.

I found myself, one day, in a village surrounded by cherry blossom trees. But I was angered by the world, frustrated by problems I could not control on my own. I had fled to this small village. Desperate to shield my heart from the world. In this village, on my first evening, I met a woman; silver hair, gold hoop earrings, a smile stretched ear to ear. And she asked me to walk with her. At first, I declined. "It is too dark," I mused.

But the woman replied, "The world is always dark; you cannot escape darkness. But you can live in it."

So, I followed.

By a bridge, connecting over a canal to the other side, the woman finally stopped.

"It is too dark," I said again. "We cannot see our way across."

But then a flicker of a flame illuminated, and the woman lit the first lantern on the path.

"We light each lantern for someone who needs kindness," she said, and she handed me a match.

"My heart is too heavy," I replied. "I don't feel like being kind tonight."

But the woman insisted.

So, reluctantly but purposefully, I lit the next lantern

and then another, and together we continued lighting the lanterns across the bridge until we had reached the other side. The bridge was now illuminated, guiding our path back home.

I stood beside the woman, looking at the bright light of the lanterns.

"Don't you see?" she said. "If you light your life with kindness, you will always be able to see your way home."

For so much of my existence, I truly
believed grace would be awarded in a light
found only in the moment between day and night

> And I searched for this moment, waiting
> wondering how so many others in the world
> could forgive themselves for all the errors
> or blunders they had made along the way

But I had been searching in all the wrong places
for while such beauty is captured in the space between
a sleeping sun and a star-filled sky—

> There is more beauty inside my heart
> where all grace begins, spreading my wings to fly.

Carry grace with you
in all the places that you seek
and all the towns that you go.

Carry it with you over every mountain
that you climb and every sea that you sail.

Carry grace through every rainstorm,
every sundrenched afternoon, every season,
and every time you fall.

Carry grace through every dark and murky
moment and into every bright and colorful
moment too.

Carry grace even when it feels heavy.

For grace makes trees grow taller,
songs sound sweeter, and days seem stronger.

I carry such grace, and I carry it for you.

Find Resilience

If you take but a moment today to think about all the miles you have come and all the work you've done, may you remind yourself of this: you are still standing, even after someone tried to hammer the life right out of you. You are still breathing, even after someone tried to knock the wind right out of your lungs. You are still smiling, dreaming, living, even after someone tried to run away with all your reasons to be resilient. You are still opening the windows and letting the sunlight in, even after someone tried to steal your hope.

It took years to find our way back.
But maybe it doesn't matter that
we drifted away from each other,
that we lost sight of what life was
like with the other, that we lost being us.
The most important thing is that,
even after everything, we eventually
found our way back to each other.

I don't know how else to tell you that you will never stop learning about who you are and all the things you can do. All the growing and the changing doesn't stop in your twenties. It carries on, in your thirties, your forties, your fifties, always just on and on. And in this time, you will say goodbye to many versions of yourself. You will bury them and cry for them and then rejoice when finding the newer versions of you. This is what it means to be human, always changing, always evolving, and still here, through it all.

Growth is not an isolated thing. When you water one plant, the soil benefits too. When you oil the motor, all the other gears turn too. When you repair the wing, the whole bird flies. Often when you sit with your mind, your heart arrives and sits too, and, together, you convince your soul there is something truly extraordinary about being you.

In a group one day sat five people and their teacher. It was a warm day, the sky dotted with cotton candy but glistening. A beautiful October day.

The teacher took a book from her bag, held it up in front of the group, and told them to pass it around in a circle. So, the first person to take the book passed it to the person on their left, and then that person passed it to their left too, and so on and so forth until the book made its way around the circle. The teacher asked the group if the book was heavy, and the group shook their heads. Of course, the book was not heavy, the teacher agreed; it is easily passed from one person to the next with very little effort.

She looked at the first person once more, this time instructing them to hold the book above their head. Hold onto it for a while, the teacher said; don't let go.

After awhile, the person grew tired.

"Can I let this go now?" they asked. "It's getting heavy; I don't think I can hold it for much longer."

"Yes," replied the teacher. "The longer you hold the book above your head, the more exhausted you become, the heavier it feels."

This is the same as all the things that keep you up at night. The longer you shoulder the weight of the world on your shoulders, the more exhausted you become, and the less strength you have. The truth of what it means to carry on lies in the way we let go of the things we cannot control.

For all the apologies you have given
for things that didn't need an apology,
for all the nights you have looked in the
mirror and struggled with your body,
for all the moments you have broken and
cried with your whole aching heart,
for all the reasons you believe you don't
deserve another day and chance to start—
know that I have been looking for you,
hoping you are loved, wanting you to thrive,
for when you are believed in, you fly,
and when you are loved, you survive.

Perhaps if we saw life for what it really was,
there would be less time filled with dread
and more time to breathe and pause,
for the truth of life is quite simply said—
even on the days when we are met with struggle
and unable to predict the moments ahead,
for all the times we fall, crash, and fumble,
there is always light at the end of the tunnel.

A few months can be a lifetime of change. It can do a lot to a person. Someone can quit their job and start a new one. They can move across the country or the world. They can buy a new car or a new house or find a new softball team to play on. They can rearrange their office, their bedroom, all the books on their bookshelf. They can find a new hobby, discover a new artist, read a new book. They can find someone new to love and to hold. A few months can be enough to heal a broken, messy heart and start again.

But sometimes a few months is not enough.

They say you can hear your heart the loudest at night; the beats pulsate through your chest as you stare at the ceiling above. It's so loud, you can hear the splitting and the breaking, as though the pain might just be big enough to swallow you.

They say it hurts more at four in the morning, when you have tossed and turned all night and your face is stained with tears. But sometimes it's nine in the morning, and you are sitting in rush hour traffic, and a song comes over the radio and it still has the same beat that matched their smile and the same lyrics that will always remind you of them, and you wind down the window for air, but you smell cinnamon, the same as their hair, and it's enough to make you miss them so much you barely notice the light turn green.

A few months might not always be enough, but it adds up over time, and suddenly there are more months between having loved and having lost, and you realize you made it to the other side in the end.

Of course, time does not heal all wounds—the wounds always remain; once you are broken, you are never the same. But you are not seeing the wound for what it is. A wound always becomes a scar. And it is scars that need time to sew together, and as they sew, they bring with them resilience and courage and silver linings.

A year ago, I had found an old cabinet in a yard sale, with rotted wood, broken handles, stained-glass panels cracked, and paint chipping all the way over. Still, I had brought it home, and as I looked at it one day, wondering how I would go about repairing all the many things wrong with it, I wondered what the cabinet had looked like before it met me. Even so, when I sanded it back, took off the stained-glass panels and all the broken handles and removed all the chipped paint, the cabinet still stood. It was still sturdy, even standing in front of me completely bare.

People are like this.

We weather over time, but underneath, at our core, we still hold our dreams, our strengths, a life lived to survive. We empower ourselves by knowing that just because time chips our skin, cracks our hearts, and sometimes breaks our morale, that does not mean we don't have the capacity to hold it together underneath.

It will always feel easier to push people away, to build walls around our hearts and guard them. It is simple to turn your back and walk in the opposite direction. But we were not made to be simple. We were made to let our stories go into the world, no matter how dark or precarious they may be. The only wrong story is the one never told.

The days turned into months
and the months into years,
and I waited for the extraordinary
to arrive on my doorstep.

Had I been older back then,
maybe a little wiser, I would have
known that the extraordinary
very rarely shows up out of the blue.

It is you, yourself, who makes the
extraordinary come to you.

A CONVERSATION WITH RESILIENCE

One night, right before the holidays, I sat in my car with Resilience. The moonlight in their hair made them appear like magic. But I knew Resilience was not magic; it would never magically appear whenever I needed it. It had been a hard year; I had lost things I never thought I would lose, and it had taken me all this time to convince Resilience to stay with me all through the night.

"I don't want you to leave," I said. "I need you more than ever."

Resilience looked at me. "I know you have lived with things you wish you hadn't," it said. "You have been handed cards you wished you were never dealt.

But you have been given these things time and time again because you do not know your own strength. You do not know your own capability."

"And what if I do now?" I replied. "If I promise to always know my strength, will the cards be different?"

But Resilience just smiled, moonlight light and feathered. "Every card is yours, no matter how light or heavy; it is always meant for you—strength will always need to be reminded."

It hardly seems fair
that someone else can
undo you,
that a total stranger can
undo all the work you
have done on yourself
with just a comment
or a remark.

But the most difficult
moments of your life
are not easily buried
with a shovel.

You cannot hide all the
things that hurt you
by simply covering them
up with concrete and rubble.

But you can learn from them
and plant strength in places
where strength doesn't often grow.

For we often surprise ourselves
with all our durability inside,
having more of it than we ever
thought we had known.

We are strangers now, but I wonder if we met somewhere on a forgotten highway when the sun was setting and beautiful, looking like the way you used to look at me, if you would remember. We were twelve years old, and we believed we could build a time machine. We spent weeks gathering materials and piled them high in the middle of the street. We were so excited at the possibility of going back in time. You could stop your dad from leaving; I could tell mine not to give away the dog. You could redo the trick on your skateboard, better and more skilled; I could stop myself from falling and getting the scar now on my knee. But, of course, the time machine never worked. Even if we so desperately wanted it to. Now I wonder if I could go back in time if I would even want to at all, knowing how much I've learned and that I am so much stronger from the fall.

We sat crossed-legged at the edge of the hill, the taste of summer still on our lips as the night ebbed away and the sun began to rise. She leaned against me, staring out into the horizon, and she said, "I don't know how to feel beautiful when there are so many out there more beautiful than me."

And I replied, "Some people find beauty in all the things they own, but this is not the kind of beauty the world deserves to see. The world should know the beauty of always rising to start a day, of putting others before yourself, and always doing our best to find our way. The world should know your strength and honesty to speak for what is right, to always reach for the stars and know love wins every fight. Even if you believe your beauty does not shine in the way you want to see, know that for all the more important reasons, you will always be the most beautiful to me."

You will understand the story one day, why it was written in the way that it was written. Why it ended the way that it ended. And you will go from having had this story as your life, and it was an entire book, to then just a page, to then a sentence, and then it will just be a name. Every now and then, you will think of this name, but the weight of it won't sit so heavily on your heart. You'll hear the name, see the name, think of the name, and that's all it will be, just a name.

If you think of your mind like a closet, you can imagine that each day you rise, you must sort through which thoughts to wear and take with you out into the world.

Even if you choose thoughts that are difficult to carry and uncomfortable to wear, every thought you have exists to remind you that you will survive.

For an outfit can always be changed, and so too can a thought. So, if you start your day with difficulty, just remember, you can always change to positivity.

I cannot pretend to understand
how we ended up here—
living in a world that teaches us
it is more important for others
to love us
than for us to love ourselves.

But there is power in the undoing
and hope in the unraveling.

So, we must undo what we were taught
and unravel the mistruths
that have been spoken,
and we must rise to teach a new truth—
how you carry yourself,
and the love you show your body, mind,
and soul, will always hold more importance
than placing your self-worth into the hands
of people you don't even know.

It was the last day of the year, a year that had felt like an entire lifetime—filled with words that had been difficult to speak and moments that I had struggled to carry. But through every step, I had made a promise to myself that when the new sun rose, I would meet the old me by the ocean and I would tell her that I was grateful for all the things she had taught me that year; I would tell her she would always be with me, a reminder of how far I had come; I would tell her there was no shame in evolving and to trust the process in moving on. So, on the very last day, I did meet her at the point where the shoreline met the sea, and as we stood side by side, watching the new sun rise, I said hello to a newer me—someone with the strength to continue every path, someone who knew that, despite every setback, she would always emerge from the dark.

Find Love

Being with you is knowing
that time will change.
We will grow older; we will
always want new things,
new adventures, new chapters.

Some years won't be the best,
and others will be the best
we've ever had.

I know that we will change
so much, sometimes it will feel
like we hardly know each other at all.

But the point is to never stop
the other from growing,
to always cherish the new chapters
and the new flowers blossoming.

I will never expect you to be anyone
other than who you want to be at
any given time.

In fact, what magical moments to see,
and how beautiful to love all the women
you choose to be.

Those little moments,
with my head on your chest
and your fingertips
drawing circles
on the base of my neck.

They are the tiny moments
you are more than my home;
you are my entire world.

You said you'll be ready soon, and I'm on your couch, counting every book on your shelf, holding roses in my hand. Time wanders by, and I'm wondering why it always takes you so long to do your hair. And suddenly all the words are gone from my lips the moment you walk into the room. Even after all this time, I still get nervous by the smell of your perfume and the touch of your hand on my shoulder. I remember every little detail, every freckle, and your heart-shaped tattoo. Every night, I dream of you and all your honey sweetness and how even just thinking about you still leaves me speechless.

If I don't often say it,
just know,
you make me feel like
floating clouds.

If I don't often remind you,
just know,
you are the person I think of
as soon as the day begins.

If I don't often make sense,
just know,
everything about you
and everything about us
always does.

I am yours when the day
breaks and sets;
I am yours when the rain
falls or the sun shines.

I am yours when the trees
rustle in song;
I am yours all night long.

I am not sure if heaven exists,
but I am sure every time
I see you, my heart beats
right out of my chest.

It was two in the morning,
and she showed up in my driveway,
told me life was about all those
magical, unexpected moments.

We drove around and she showed
me all her favorite places:
the wharf that overlooked the bay,
the bookstore with the floating
bookshelves in the window,
the coffee shop with the fairy
lights in the alleyway.

And I showed her all my favorite songs,
the ones that reminded me of her,
and we kissed, and nothing in my life
had ever felt like it could be forever.

You mean so much to me.

If there is one thing that
can stand the test of time,
make it through all the ups
and all the downs of life,
it's that little piece of my
heart belonging to you.

Even if we were to ever
go days without speaking,
years without touching,
a lifetime without holding,

I would still carry you in my heart.

The universe feels unending
when I look at you.

Every star brighter from
the day we met.

The smile never fades when
I am thinking of you.

The beat of my heart
always doubles every time
I am held by you.

All these memories to outlive
time, I suppose you could say;
the love story never ends
when it comes to you.

The first time I saw you, it was as though I had never seen beauty before. The first time we spoke, it was as though I had never had a real conversation before. The first time we kissed, it was as though I had never kissed anyone else before. How you do what you do, it makes my life feel as though I am doing everything for the first time again. As though I am reliving all the best and beautiful moments over and over again.

I wish that I could undo all the chaos someone caused your heart. I wish I could undo all the hurt you felt or the way you were taught that love was nothing more than heartache and agony. I wish I could undo the way you were made to believe you'll never be deserving of love, or that you will always be left, or that you are just a forgotten building at the end of an abandoned street and there isn't a soul who could love a heart so weak. I can't undo what happened in the past, but I can arrive on your doorstep with three things: a watering can, to remind you that flowers can grow once more; a compass, to remind you that if I were to ever leave, it would be to the next adventure we'd have together; and a match, to remind you that, despite how others have diminished your flame, your fire will learn to burn again.

There was never
any choice.
You were gravity,
and I was pulled to you.

I like to think the beat
of my heart is in sync
with yours,
as though we are
two harmonies
entwined together.

When you strip everything away, atom by atom, and you are just looking at a person, heart to heart, soul to soul, you realize that we aren't all that different. We still want someone to love us, hold us, care for us in a way that we love them, hold them, care for them too. I think that is why love will always mean so much. Because love doesn't choose whom it wants and whom it doesn't want. Love doesn't measure people based on their flaws or perfections or the color of their skin or all their hopes and dreams. Love exists to remind us we are all connected, from the sky to the sea and everything in between.

You came along and turned my whole world upside down. Now I'm spending time looking at your golden hair in the wind, cherry lipstick, open road, your hand to hold. I'm missing all the exits just to watch that sun go down, so we can stay a little longer. You've got that smile on, the one you only wear with me, and if I feel safe anywhere, it's right here. It's golden hour, so let's just keep going, see all the miles that stretch between the beaches and the forests and the mountains and skylines. I just want all my time to be filled with you, because, one thing is for sure, I can't imagine any day without you.

The garden was beautiful that afternoon; I met you by the fountain after you had called and said you needed to talk. And you had looked at me, told me that for all the stars in the sky and the years in forever, you would love me. That it had always been me, from the beginning of time. So when you closed the gap between us, took my face in your hands, and kissed me, I knew there would never be any space between us again, because you were the sun and I was the moon and together we were the fireworks that filled that afternoon.

We were on the couch, watching old movies with glasses of wine, and she looked at me, told me she wanted to share all the deepest parts of her mind. And I can't count all the times I've closed my eyes, breathed in deep, thanked every star she's someone I can keep. Her eyes are always lit up, like she has the universe in her eyes. I know we didn't meet on accident, because her love is what I think magic is.

All I have to do is look at you, and I just want you to stay the night and dream with me. You say my name and my heart melts; how it has thought of you in all its space and folds, I can't imagine it belonging to anyone else. I see your face in every color and your smile in every wonder. I just know I can love you like no other. Promise me I'm yours, because I know I'll never leave. I'll be all that you need; your forever is everything to me.

I can't promise things will always be easy, this forever we have chosen. I can't promise to always know what to do, to be bold or triumphant or brazen. Some days will be more difficult than others, some years lost that we can never get back. We will see both the best and the worst in each other; sometimes we'll argue, and we won't even want to be around one another. We will fight, and it might be about silly little things, like whose turn it is to do the laundry, or the dishes, or the lawn. But on the other side is the way your laughter fills every room, how I have your shoulder and you have mine to cry on. The weekends, dancing in the living room and sharing a bottle of wine. Cooking dinner together, walking the dogs, being the first person I see in the morning and the last at night. I'm not always sure what will come next, but I just know every time you smile, I lose my breath. I just know that you are the most beautiful, weirdest, silliest, smartest person I have met, and forever means I gave you my word; I'll cross the universe to give you all that you deserve.

And when I talk
of the things I am
most passionate about

or the things that
bring me joy
or the reasons
I wake up every day,

I find myself talking
more and more of you.

They say the heart creates enough energy
to drive a truck twenty miles every day,
and in a lifetime that is the same as driving
to the moon and back.

So, when I tell you that I would cross miles
for you and that I love you to the moon and back,
I mean this with all the energy in my heart
for the rest of my life.

I swear that I never lived before you.

If you want to be here forever,
I hope that you'll know your smile
is something I'll always need.

As long as I have you with me,
the same way the night has the day,
I know everything will be okay.

You reached for me
and closed the space between us,
holding my face in your hands.

And when you kissed me,
I couldn't remember if it lasted
a minute or an hour, but I dreamed
of stars in every color, and I knew
I never wanted to kiss another.

What I love most
is that even in the silence,
I know that we are talking.

We speak in the rhythm of our pulse,
the electricity between our fingers,
the dreams shared in every breath,
the love between our souls.

You start by learning
how someone wants
to be loved, and you
love them in this way
for all their life.

Our love can be messy, and sometimes it's hard to compromise, to sacrifice our own needs for each other's. But our love is also wrapped in simplicity. The way your hand brushes mine as we pass in the hall, how you look at me over dinner some nights and I just know I have it all. The way you laugh, how it makes me laugh even more. The way you smile into my lips sometimes, right after I have said I like your hair today; or the way you did your eyes; or how safe I feel with you, no matter how fast time flies. It's all the simple gestures, the soft moments: they are all the things that make you and me worth it.

I knew I truly loved you, because it was a gray sort of day and you walked into the room, tangled hair, one sock higher than the other, oldest sweater in your favorite color—you looked at me with that smile, unphased and unconcerned, and yet, in that moment, it felt as though the sun had returned.

The things that I love most are the things that bring me joy. An extra marshmallow or two in my hot chocolate, hiking a mountain to watch the sunrise, falling asleep on the beach in the late, late afternoon sun. Three perfectly timed backflips on a trampoline, the feeling of bare feet on grass or sand or carpet, looking up at a night sky full of the brightest stars I've ever seen. To feel joy and peace of mind is to be in love, and to be in love with life is the greatest joy you will ever find.

If I could see you every sunrise,
I'd bring your favorite coffee,
tell you the sun would be brighter
and the day a little better
because we were always together.

If I could see you every month,
I'd show you all the little places
that meant the world to me,
tell you they now meant so much more,
for a place is just a memory to share
with someone you absolutely adore.

If I could see you every year,
I'd wrap my arms around you,
tell you for all the time we've missed
and for everywhere I went,
I'd thought of you often and seen you
in all the dreams I'd dreamt.

And yet, I only see you in pockets of time,
spread out over calls and texts and waiting,
always wondering what it would mean if we
did not live on opposite sides of the sea.

Still, today, I wanted you to know—
I think of you in every sunrise and in all
the places that I love; I think of every coffee,
dream, and hug. For the simple truth of life,
despite all the things we've been through,
is that there is nothing quite like the joy
of a beautiful friend like you.

Don't you hear it, the way a melody erupts from line to line? Don't you see it, all the ways it unfolds, reaching for your heart and mine? We are always chasing the grandest of things—big dreams, the best success, the glory in life. But we forget the power in simplicity, the beauty of a door to your soul opening, anticipating a new thought, changed from simple words on a page. A story inspires another story, a paragraph imprints a journey on your heart, a handful of sentences sparks a conversation from silence; it is a bridge connecting you to me and all the ways we wish our hopes and dreams to be heard. Don't you think that is the most beautiful thing in the world?

I have always thought of healing as the soul breaking the heart, for the free spirit of the heart does not always understand the clarity of the mind, and when they do not see page to page, it is the soul that splits in two. But as fragmented as the soul becomes, it is still beautiful. You can break your own heart and tear your soul apart, but the space you create for your healing will be the greatest act of love you give yourself.

There is a reason for every moment,
every thought, every memory—
how a picture ended up on a wall,
how a song ended up on an album,
how a poem ended up on a page.

And behind every reason is a love story;
perhaps my favorite is the story of how
you fell in love with life
and life fell in love with you.

It is the *way* she loves me—
with all her energy
and her whole soul.

She loves me in the way
she loves every new day.

She loves me even if
we are doing something
as small and as mundane
as sitting on the balcony
with two cups of coffee,
watching the birds
beyond the fence line.

This is how I know
there isn't anyone else
in the whole wide world
I would want to call mine.

It was always her.

And I have been there. I was younger once, a little naive, a little lost in a world that always felt one step ahead of where I was. I thought I knew what love was; I thought I knew how to love and how to be loved in return. But the truth was, I needed to meet all the wrong people before I met the right person. I needed to lose myself before I knew the way I wanted to be loved. I needed to learn and to grow and to stop wishing away life before it had happened to me. I needed to absorb every moment as it happened, watch more sunrises, feel the ocean air in my hair, and let go of the things holding me back. And I knew that one day I would find a love that made sense. I knew one day I would find someone who didn't try to change me, who was honest and faithful and wanted all the very best things for me. I knew I would find someone who I could truly love and who would love me back equally.

One day, I am going to buy you a house, a place to call our home. It will have a long driveway lined with trees, a garden, a swing, and it'll be our own. Maybe we'll have a couple kids, at least a few more dogs, and I want an old jukebox so every now and then we can dance to our wedding song. One day, when the sun sets over our home, I'll look at you, remind you that every breath I take is to give you the happiness that you deserve, and our story won't ever have an end, because our love will always stretch to the ends of the universe.

And then one day
someone walks into your life,
a total stranger, and they
become so important to you.

And while you've known them
such a short time,
you feel you have loved
them for a lifetime.

Under the surface
of the sea,
a whale can hear
another whale's song
for miles and miles.

This is how I imagine
my love for you.

Even if I cannot see you,
we are still connected by
a rhythm of devotion.

I will still hear the drum
of your heart
and the song of our love
across the entire ocean.

And here is what I know: I know that for all the times you have been sad, you will have many more times when you are happy. I know that you will find a love that reaches for you through the darkness and holds your hand. I know that you will find what inspires you, what drives you, what motivates all your goals and plans. I know that you will learn just how much your story begins with your soul and the way you nurture it, heal it, replenish it in the moments you don't feel whole. I know that you will find your people, the kind who lift you up, support you in everything you do. I know that you will find someone who loves you for everything that you are, who accepts you, cherishes you, dreams of you in the brightest colors the world has known. I know how beautiful—magic even—it is, the way love can bring us home. I know that you will wake up one day with such love in your heart, and I know you'll be okay.

Find Purpose

Believe me when I say there are many moments in which I do not wish to put pen to page, for I have run out of all the things I want to say. And in these times, when words seem redundant, repetitive, or incomplete, I often think of my purpose and the will of my heart every time it beats. Purpose is a peculiar thing—when you are young, you feel you have purpose for many things, and then you grow, and these things start to narrow, and you realize sometimes purpose changes, wherever you end up and wherever you go. But even if I do not always have the words, I understand the purpose of life—and it exists in the things that while small in nature bring you such joy—like beating the high score on the arcade machine, the smell of fresh flowers as you walk in a door, the way your dog rolls in the long-overgrown grass, how infectious such joy is when someone laughs. So, I suppose, even in the absence of words, purpose still exists, as surely as salt in the sea, the sun in the sky, and the melody of songbirds.

I will tell you something, about a time that will arrive for you—unexpectedly, risen from the very depths of all that you thought you were—a shift in who you are, so much so, it awakens senses you never knew you had. You will be reminded of your purpose, of your strength to scale mountains, of your courage to light up the sky, of all the reasons you belong to this world. And you will carry this feeling and take back all the roads that were stolen from you.

We were only new, but I had this renewed purpose for life. How someone crashes into you with such force you are blinded by all that they are is still a mystery to me.

One day, I looked at you and whispered that I was jealous of all those who had come before me—they had more time with you, more kisses, more hand holding, more listening to their names held delicately on your lips—I had wished that it had been my lips, my hands, my love instead.

And yet you just smiled and said, "But you'll spend always with me."

She ran alongside the river,
returning the water home
to the ocean.
She fed the birds, watching
them take flight one by one.
She counted the lampposts
every morning on her walk,
checking the light, making
sure the street would always
be filled with light.

She called out to the moon,
and they shared their secrets.
The sun always reached her,
even through the clouds,
kissing the tops of her shoulders,
leaving freckles in secret places
only meant for love.

She had courage and admiration
for the everyday, ordinary things—
she was magic, filled with purpose,
and she was worth it, for this
I am unequivocally certain.

Once upon a time, there was a girl who loved a girl; they lived in a town with a single mountain, in a house on the fringes of the woods. It was here they spoke of many things, of dreams and hopes and possibilities. What it was to dream, to have purpose, what it meant to look at each other and see an entire universe in the pockets of one another's soul.

It meant everything—you mean everything.

We were dizzy on sunshine and kisses from the sky, having danced in the sun-shower and collapsing on the hill. You looked at me and said, "Do you know the most beautiful thing about life?"

And I said, "I do not know."

And you replied, "We are here. Feel the earth." You smiled, and your hands reached for the blades of grass and the soil beneath.

I did too; I reached for the earth, to soak in every moment, every memory. The soft whispering of the trees, the sweetness of the apple trees, the soft touch of light from above.

You said, "We lose our soul when we do not love each moment; we gain it entirely when we do."

I loved the moment entirely, and the world melted away with you.

The whole universe melded together to create you;
the stars pulled together, the sun brought warmth,
the moon shone brighter, and the planets aligned.

The whole sky erupted just for you.

It's just the way we are—we forget things. Memories overlap sometimes; dreams replace things that never really happened. The world plows on, and we lose ourselves in the crowd. But I hope, even in the darkness, you never forget your worth. Even when you forget where to find it, even if you forget how to hold on to it, know that is it still there, waiting for you to embrace it.

You have spent all these years trying to place
the pieces of yourself into the wrong puzzle.

But so have I—

It is perhaps the greatest mystery of our lives:
the puzzle we want is not composed of the
pieces we are given.

So, we are left unsure of the things we desire,
the person we want to be, the dreams we seek.

Who am I, where will I go, what will I become?

But we have lost sight of the bigger picture and
what the puzzle really means.

For this reason, I have been trying to think of
every little piece with gratitude rather than as
things that will distract me from what I want in life.

And when you have gratitude, life doesn't
become so much of a puzzle anymore—

Because the bigger picture is right in front of you.
Your pieces have always fit together exactly as the
universe had intended.

I will take all the parts of you
     that you are too afraid to trust
     and I will place them over my heart
     so you may see the way each beat
     trusts all of you completely

I will hold all the parts of you
     that you are too afraid to love
     and I will wrap them into my soul
     so you may see how my entire being
     loves knowing you are here with me

I will admire all the parts of you
     that you are too afraid to uncover
     and I will bring them into my eyes
     so every time we look at each other
     you will know the beauty I see in you

You are more than likes and comments and views on a story. It is easy to become trapped inside such a void. And in your frailer moments, you wonder, how did this happen, that my entire sense of worth is dependent on people I have never even met? When did my purpose become so intertwined with strangers on the internet?

And this is my note to you: the world inside your heart is far greater and more beautiful than a comment or a like cares to know. And if you stopped but for a moment to realize life goes on with or without the next post, you might remember you still have purpose despite the things that haunt you the most.

You will be walking down the street one day, and you will feel lighter. And you will wonder what happened. Did time freeze and lead you to this new sense of belonging, or did it speed up and you missed the place of purpose in which you have arrived? Either way, you will consider the thoughts others have of you less than the thoughts you have about yourself. And it will be freeing. Of course, like most, every now and then, you'll get that feeling deep in your heart, the doubt, the insecurity, the wondering if you are good enough, but it's such a small and fleeting feeling—it's over before it has time to grow. And, instead, you'll be sitting across from someone years younger than you, and you'll smile and say, "You'll get here eventually, just so you know."

Do you see me here
        pressed against this wall,
        legs shaking, eyes wandering?
        Do you know of my existence
        or my name at all?

Will you listen to me here
        for all the things I have to say
        and all the purpose that I seek
        of my ambitions every day,
        all the doubt I have every week?

Is there anybody out there
        who will stop and notice
        this lonely flower on the wall
        hoping to grow a garden
        instead of feeling so small?

You look at the night sky
and at every single dot—
a star burning miles away.
And every dot its own galaxy,
and every galaxy holding
persistence, dreams, and love.

So, if for every dot you see
you can imagine all the billions
of people in this world and all
the galaxies inside them, filled
with purpose and filled with life,

Then, you are allowed to love
whom you love and want what you
want—you are here to shine.

I have spent my life running—through old towns, across oceans, immersed in people, the woods, the ocean shores, restaurants with dimly lit lights. I have been running, refusing to ever look back, always focused on the mile in front of me. I have discarded my heart to find my soul; I have ignored my mind in the hopes the thoughts will change on their own one day. And yet, in all this running, I have been unable to outrun myself. You can run from cities, you can run to corners of the earth so far away from the place you call home, but you cannot outrun yourself. You cannot outrun the imbalance between your thoughts, the beat of your heart, the longing in your soul.

There was a defining moment, and I looked in the mirror and I apologized. I apologized to my eyes, for I have never loved the color. I apologized to my hands, for I have always thought they were too small. I apologized to my smile, for I have always tried to hide it, too focused on a single crooked tooth rather than what a smile truly means, that I feel joy. I apologized to my legs, for I have always criticized their size and forgotten that they have carried me miles and miles. I apologized to my arms, to my stomach, to my chest, to my whole body, for I have not been its friend for quite some time, when despite all that I say it has always been mine.

"I will get to it," you say. "I will find the time."

But you do not ask "When" and you do not answer with "Now."

You say, "After."

And it's always after—after the sun goes down, after the working week, after the children grow up, after the year turns to the next.

Never now and always after.

But "after" will not always exist, and "now" will always change until it is no more.

Don't you feel what I feel for you? You are deserving of a life worth living for.

It is always a war between the mind and body—
I wish that I could take all your insecurities
and all the reasons you don't think you are beautiful
and press them between the pages of a book, like flowers,
so they will become art to you instead of such darkness.
Your mind was made for strength and your body made for love.

In a small fishing town, a young child lived with his grandfather. All winter long, it had rained and rained, and as he had sat on the living room floor by the fire and dreamed of learning how to sail, he begged his grandfather to teach him. And so, the grandfather had agreed, but on the promise that the boy understood—a lesson is to only ever be taught at the right time.

When the weather warmed, the child asked if they could take one of the boats out into the water and start his lessons. The sea was now perfect, still, crystal clear. But the grandfather shook his head and told the boy he must wait, that it was not the right time. The days went on, one after the other, and the boy continued to ask, and the grandfather continued to say no. And the boy grew frustrated. "I am never going to learn to sail," he said. "Never!"

Until one day, a storm billowed beyond the horizon and waves became a little bumpy and the sky a little windy. "Now," said the grandfather, his eyes glinting, "we will sail."

"In this?" replied the boy. "How can we possibly sail in this? We should have gone when the weather was calmer and steady. It was much safer then."

The grandfather shook his head. "You will never learn by staying still, and you will never understand if everything is made easy. This is not the purpose of life.

It is only *through* the storm you find the courage to continue and the understanding of clear skies ahead."

THE END

An ending placed in a page of a book that is not really the end—perhaps this is the purpose. Endings are with us, from the beginning, somewhere in the middle, all the way to the very finale. Things and people and places end all the time, and yet the page, with or without you, will always move to the next.

I trust that
there is purpose,
in all the things I feel.

Even if the pain
takes years to heal.

Even if the journey
feels impossible to
explain.

There have been moments
when all I could think about
was sinking into my bed and
never returning.

That if I closed my eyes and
wished hard enough, I would
be swallowed whole.

That I would be done with all
the thoughts, of always asking
where, to whom, and to what
do I belong.

What is the reason for me.

I have wished this many times:
I have dreamed I am a burning,
bright star, exploding and then
disappearing.

The universe drinks me in,
and I am home again.

And yet, despite this,
I still wake,
and I still rise.

Sixty minutes in an hour, one hundred and sixty-eight hours in a week, three hundred and sixty-five days in an average year, ten years in a decade; and they will not stop. These hours, weeks, months, and years will not pause for you or for me. They will continue piling on top of each other, day after day, month after month, year after year, until suddenly there is an entire lifetime laid out in front of you. And you will wonder where it all went. Where did these beautiful, precious days go? And more than that, you will wonder what you did with all the time—so maybe we shouldn't sit on the sidelines. What if we tried to do it together, leave the sidelines, run into life, chase after every moment? I am sure we can find our becoming.

The universe looked on as the earth descended into the storm—and in its wake, the people lost their purpose and their will to carry on.

In a tiny town only accessible by boat, at the very edge of a crumbling street, there lived a girl. As the storm took hold, the town became silent, and the girl was forced to retreat behind walls.

For many months, all she knew was isolation and bad news.

Horrors that reached every part of the globe from a storm that did not care about race or religion or who was who. And even if the fear spread to all the parts of her soul, the girl believed in a day the world would take back what the storm stole.

For even through disaster, the world would come to find that life goes on—and despite the end of many things, this was not the end of humankind.

One night, at a quarter past two, she crept on tiptoes out to the pond in the corner of the yard to speak to the universe and ask for three wishes she desperately needed. As she looked at the reflection upon the water's surface, and the moonlight kissed her skin, she asked the universe for her first wish: "Please help us begin again."

So, begin again she did, and she started with small steps, like choosing to spend an hour in the sunlight and searching for answers in its depth.

The second wish was patience for all those who chose entitlement over togetherness, for to be patient with those who cannot see the right path to follow is to be patient in the face of anger, despite all the times frustration is difficult to swallow.

And the third wish was for peace of mind, for while life will never carry on quite the same, carry on it must, for all the things to come and all the things we wish to reclaim.

Find Faith

If I could write you a note
with all the things I know to be true,
this is what the note would say
and how I would reassure you—
"Life is only an anchor if you don't
remind yourself to breathe,
and sometimes there are no answers
for why people leave.
But you are worthy of more things
than you ever dream to believe,
and there is more hope in life
than you let yourself think,
even on the days that feel like
they were made to sink.
It can be difficult, knowing when
to speak and when to ask for help,
but your story is not a story
that deserves to be left on the shelf.
More important than all the things
you fear is where you place your faith;
just know you will always belong here
and your story is not one that can be erased."

The uphill battle feels as though
it may never end, and this is because
it won't.

Just because you get to the top of the
hill does not mean there is not another
hill to climb. It does not mean that it
won't rain on top of the hill or you won't
slip and fall, tumbling right back down
to where you started.

Just because you can see the silver lining
does not mean you don't have to do all the
work it takes to get there and that this work
will never stop.

But is it the refusal to not climb that makes
life easier to dance with. Despite having one
battle after another, you go in swinging and
charging forward, because you have faith.

Having hope is better than feeling hopeless.

And believe me,
for it is the truth,
those years without you,
I thought of you often.
I hoped for you always.
I missed you for forever.

If the earth and I could sit
in the center of a room,
I would fold her into my arms
and tell her
I love all the ways
in which she blooms.

I'd tell her I was sorry for all the
days I ignored the beauty in a
sunrise or the thrill of a storm.

I'd tell her I have been paying
more attention to the sky, the trees,
and all the little bees.

I'd tell her if we worked together,
then surely we can strengthen
how mindful we are of the
mountains, lakes, and seas.

And if the earth could speak back to me,
I am sure she would agree that nothing
in life is ever guaranteed, so look after
every heart, every creature and soul alike,
take note of every piece of magic glistening
in sunlight.

For if we don't start now and step toward
being brave, then years from now
there will be nothing left to save.

Time is a wonderful thing—
it awards perspective,
it asks for acknowledgment,
it brings healing,
it offers forgiveness.

Give yourself time to
see things more clearly.

Give yourself time to
acknowledge your pain,
your trauma, your ache.

Give yourself time to
focus on your healing.

Give yourself time to
forgive a world that hurt you
or the mistakes you made.

Give yourself time to
find yourself again.

I have faith that your heart
has known my heart before,
that sometime in between
then and now, years ago and more,
I made a single wish on the
biggest and brightest star
that, for every new life,
I'd be right where you are.

There we were, after years of not being together, after all this time that had passed in our lives. You were different, but you were the same. I didn't know you, but I still knew you. And all the anger, frustration, and hurt disappeared the moment I saw you, and all that I had in my heart was this wonder of how we could have gone on so long without each other. But maybe we needed to spend all this time apart. Maybe we needed to move on with our lives, find new paths, seek new roads without the other, navigate waters as our own captains. Maybe it taught us something to hope for in this world. I know what it taught me; I'll never let you go again.

It felt like everything in me doubled. My heartbeat, my breathing, my need to be closer to you. I wanted double every moment, double the hours, double the years, and double the lifetimes. It was never enough to look at you once, to be with you once, not when you split my heart in half and fused one part to yours. I had hoped for you for so long that when you finally arrived, my life was no longer mine but ours.

I hope that when you count down toward midnight to welcome in a new year, you stop for a moment and remember all the things you hold dear. For life is not always about making lists of resolutions and all the things you wish to do; instead, it's about finding gratitude in all the reasons you are, are you. So, when you start every new year and raise a glass with glee, have faith in this very simple truth: you are right where you are always meant to be.

They say we all have a breaking point,
a moment every single wall caves in—
they say it's the moment we lose our voice
and forget to listen deep within.

At my lowest, I struggled to find the light,
and even though the sun bookends each day,
all I could see were the shadows of the night.

But every morning, I chose to rise;
I considered a hopeful thing to say—
that despite days filled with gray skies,
me being me is enough reason to stay.

She had learned how to cry quietly, under covers or in the shower, where no one would notice and no one would ask questions. And if anyone asked, she would always respond that it was nothing. But, of course, it wasn't nothing. She was an ocean, always arriving on the shore but never being able to stay, always being pulled back to the depths of darkness. Every loss is met with a gain, every grief met with happiness, every fear met with understanding. Yet it was the loss, the grief, and the fear that she focused on; unreasonable, she knew, but she could not control the darkness, no matter how much light she was given. This is the thing of such darkness; it will convince you to lose hope in yourself—and you will, time and time again. But no matter how many times the ocean arrives on the shore and then leaves, know that I will remain, waiting in moonlight for you to arrive again—I have faith in you.

It was the month I lost someone I loved, and I did not know how to describe the grief inside. I tried to write of how I felt, in every journal, notebook, or napkin I could find. But the words did not come, and the pain only grew. So desperate for relief, I decided to meet with Poetry at the very back of a café and at the end of a lonely street. I waited all morning, until Poetry finally arrived and sat down in front of me. I asked, "Where do I go when I do not have the words to write?"

Poetry studied me with heavy eyes for quite some time and said, "You have lost the words because you have forgotten what exists on each and every line."

And I looked back, "I do not know what you mean."

But Poetry just reached out a hand, took mine in theirs, and said, "I am really just a feeling that has found a way to speak, so if you cannot find me now and again, just remember I exist in your heart and breathe through your pen."

The most beautiful parts of your life, the real happiness, the true stuff, will be many small, nameless moments. They are never explosive; even if the explosive moments do matter, it will always be about the everyday, little sparks. The laugh of the love of your life; the first time your child learns to ride a bike; dancing the night away with your friends; a sunrise, bright and beautiful; a glass of wine while on vacation; staring out at an ocean view. But perhaps the most you will ever feel filled is from that whisper through the dark, saying, "Everything is okay, my love. I've got you."

I do not want a life
that is wild and
filled with chaos.

I want a life that is soft
and gentle and filled with
warmth.

As though I am the sun,
finding my way back after
days of rain.

I don't want a life filled
with insecurities or unanswered
questions.

I want to be a home that you feel
safe in—I hope so much for this.

We meet some people
and we only cross paths
so they may teach us
how to be better.

They remind us of all
the beautiful things that
exist inside us; they prove
we were not a mistake.

And even long after they
are gone, we are still left
with a greater understanding.

That sometimes the universe
gives us people disguised as hope.

One morning, I stood in front of the mirror, and I asked my body what our goals for the week were. How many days would we exercise, how many times would we consider what we ate, how many weights would we lift, how many mornings would we meditate. So many variables, so many moments of consideration, reflection, planning, and preparation.

"What are our goals?" I asked, reaching for my shoes. "What are we going to focus on today?" And my body replied, "Do you suppose one could be that you just love me, no matter what I weigh?"

I wish I had understood this better when I was younger—
that humans do, in fact, emit light. We glow, faintly, not
seen to the naked eye but still there. If I had known back
then that I could exist in this world as light, then perhaps I
would not have found so many ways to stay in the darkness.
If I had known that all the joy, the happiness, and healing
already lived inside of me, then I would not have spent so
many days searching for it. We are born to illuminate in
darkness; we are born to find our way.

If the year taught us anything, it's that, despite our readiness, things don't always go to plan. I won't always know what to do in the moments all eyes are on me, and I won't always know what to say in the times words are needed most. I won't always know what way to go, ideas to follow, or dreams to pursue. I won't have all the answers, and no matter how much I try, I cannot predict tomorrow. But the year also taught us that kindness still exists and strength finds its way to us, even in the moments we feel truly amiss. As long as we focus our eyes ahead and open every new door we find, then the year that was is just that, a year to leave behind. The year taught us a significant lesson—to believe in hope is to start with what's inside, for when *you* have hope and *I* have hope, then together we can do anything: together we will survive.

Some old friends—perhaps you have heard of them; one is called Fox and the other Owl—met one night when the stars hung low and the forest became alive.

Feeling all sorts of things, from lost to misunderstood, Fox had traveled to their friend, who always listened, as all friends should.

Fox turned to Owl and wondered out loud, "Where do I go when there is no more road left to travel?"

And Owl pondered, for it was a good question indeed. Where *do* we go in our greatest moment of need?

And so replied Owl, "Well, the journey is never really over. You return as someone different, a little more grown, no matter how many times you walk the same road."

Fox thought on this for quite a while, as the fireflies danced and the stars looked down with a smile.

Yes, thought Fox, for what dear Owl had said was true: no matter how many times you walk the same road, at the very beginning to the very end, you always become someone new.

I was once asked, "Why do poets write of the same things, only arranged differently and dressed in new ways? You must spend your whole lives writing the same poem."

While at first I was taken aback, I soon came to smile, for, yes, there is nothing I can say that you would find new, but the truth of life is in the knowing that, despite all the miles we travel, we never do stop growing.

This is what I know—I know that the sun will still rise every morning, if we can see it or not. The moon too. And I know that the stars will always be beautiful, just like you. There will always be a mountain to climb, a path to walk, an ocean to cross, always miles from where you started and miles to where you are headed. And even if you feel there are things you already know, you will always need to be reminded of hope wherever you are and wherever you go.

You will build your home time and time again. In every facet, corner, moment of your life, you are always building and always shaping yourself. There will be another storm one day; it could be worse, it could be better, it could be somewhere in between—but the storm will come again. The way we survive is by knowing such times will always arrive but they do not mean the end. Instead, we look for courage to start again, for grace in how we hold ourselves, for support in those around us, and strength and resilience in the way we carry on. And we take all these things, we surround them in love and faith, and together we build ourselves once more, for the key to life is remembering there is always purpose in spite of the storm.

Thank you for reading this book.

I hope you enjoyed reading it as much as I enjoyed writing it. You can stay up to date with all my latest news and projects via my website, www.peppernell.com.

Feel free to write to me via courtney@pepperbooks.org.

Pillow Thoughts app now available on iOS and Android stores worldwide and on all devices—download yours today for your daily poetry!

Andrews McMeel Publishing
a division of Andrews McMeel Universal
1130 Walnut Street, Kansas City, Missouri 64106

www.andrewsmcmeel.com

22 23 24 25 26 RR2 10 9 8 7 6 5 4 3 2 1

ISBN: 978-1-5248-7211-3

Library of Congress Control Number: 2022936485

Editor: Patty Rice
Art Director: Diane Marsh
Designer: Rhea Wyss
Production Editor: Elizabeth A. Garcia
Production Managers: Cliff Koehler and Tamara Haus

Illustrations by Justin Estcourt